The Unveiling

The Unveiling

CURT SIMMONS

DPI
DISCIPLESHIP
PUBLICATIONS
INTERNATIONAL

One Merrill Street
Woburn, Mass. 01801
1-800-727-8273

The Unveiling
©1995 by Discipleship Publications International
One Merrill Street, Woburn, MA 01801

Cover Design: Nora Robbins
Cover Photo: Tony Stone Images, © Richard Kaylin

Printed in the United States of America

ISBN 1-884553-59-1

DEDICATION

To my wife Patty,
Thanks for being my best friend.
Your sense of humor brings me much-needed sanity.
Your selfless love brings me much-needed security.
Thanks for letting God use you for the last 15 years to
"straighten out my messes."
Your pure heart and pursuit of God have always been an
upward call. I love you with all my heart.

And to our parents,
Vern and Priscilla Simmons
and
Everitt and Catherine Hatfield.
Thank you for helping to make my life and
my family's a complete joy.

I love you all.

CONTENTS

PREFACE

*N*othing in life is more important than knowing God. It is my conviction that our attitudes, decisions and ultimately our joy-level are directly proportionate to our understanding of who he is. My goal is simply to point you back to your Creator—thus clearing your thoughts, encouraging proper and godly decisions, and helping you find the happiness God so desperately desires for every human being.

Writing a book is a scary undertaking. Writing a book about the nature of God is frightening. What if I miss? What if I miscommunicate? What if I miss, you agree with me, and we miss out together? Nevertheless, the topic must be discussed because the present picture of God in much of our world is rather disgusting.

So much has had to happen to bring this book to you. God has kept me breathing for 35 years. He has been more than patient with me and has not punished me as my sins deserve. Though involved in a tremendous amount of sin in both high school and college, God in his "never be able to understand" love put people and situations together, perfectly orchestrating an opportunity for me to become his child. I am forever thankful he helped me to accept his call. For the past 13 years, I have made it my goal to know him, listen to him and love him.

I have had tremendous help along the way to continue in this quest and deal with my "present-day" problems and sins. Thank you, Bob Tuerck, for having the courage to ask me to get involved. Thanks to Preston Shepherd for being up-front from the outset, showing me nothing but Bible to destroy my false hopes, and then teaching me to be a friend to the hurting. To Kenny Jacobs, for showing me true humility and how to work together as a team. To Gordon Ferguson, who was my first "extra" dad. Thanks for all your counseling and belief in me. To Gregg Marutzky, who remained patient while I remained critical—who taught me that toughness and tenderness together are expected and attainable. To John Causey, who greatly encouraged me when I needed it most. To Ron Brumley and John Mannel, true elders in God's church who, more than they realize, have kept me in the flock by their teaching—but mostly by their example. To Ron Drabot who, more than anyone I know, strives to be like Jesus and wears out his knees for his people. These and others have been my teachers: men determined to follow New Testament direction to make sure men like myself are not acting on their own, but are being taught and guided on life's tough, narrow road.

But thanks mostly to my wife. Patty exploded on the scene May 16, 1980, just two days before Mt. St. Helens exploded for the world to see. A college friend and I were out looking for some Friday night folly and met Patty and her friend, who were just in front of us in a slow, long line, all of us waiting to order burgers and shakes. Little did I know that at the time, God was ordering my life. Only a breath away was a sweet, God-fearing seventeen-year-old who would encourage me to begin my quest to not just acknowledge God, but pursue him. Though initially it was Patty I pursued most, I ultimately found what I was needing—a great woman and an even greater God.

The 14th of 15 children, Patty has been a pillar of strength during our time together. Despite the death of loved ones and personal disappointments, she remains happy and headed in the right direction. With her, I am a better man. Without her, this book would not be.

As you read, you will find many quotes from the Bible. In some cases I have discussed the context; in others I have not. However, in all the examples used, especially in Chapters Seven, Eight and Nine, reading the entire chapter or book in the Bible to discover the context will only strengthen the main point of this book—God is amazing!!

You will notice only limited discussion on Jesus Christ. What do I believe about Jesus? He is the Son of God, Wonderful Counselor, Mighty God, Prince of Peace and Savior of the world. Without him and his blood, no man may enter the kingdom of heaven. The overall purpose of this book, however, is to unveil God the Father. My desire, in the near future, is to write another book looking at the biblical Christ and comparing him to the 20th century stereotypes that leave many undesirous of pursuing him.

Please keep in mind this book will not solve your problems—only inform you more about the problem-solver. This book will not get you to heaven—only point you to the carpenter currently working on your mansion. This book will not make you happy, only introduce you to the author of the smile.

For each reader whose life is changed in some way as a result of this book, all thanks be directed to the One who gives you each and every breath and who can also ultimately take it away.

Chapter One

The Unveiling

"But whenever anyone turns to the Lord, the veil is taken
away. Now the Lord is the Spirit, and where the Spirit
of the Lord is, there is freedom. And we, who with
unveiled faces all reflect the Lord's glory, are being
transformed into his likeness with ever-increasing glory,
which comes from the Lord, who is the Spirit"
(2 Corinthians 3:16-18).

"And even if our gospel is veiled, it is veiled to those
who are perishing. The god of this age has blinded the
minds of unbelievers, so that they cannot see the light of
the gospel of the glory of Christ, who is the image of God"
(2 Corinthians 4:3-4).

"...And they all lived happily ever after."

The last-line legacy in the fairy tale world is really nothing more than a huge lie in the real world. The truth is, most people are only *hoping* for happiness. People living with seemingly solution-less problems. People separated from God with few hints on how to find him. People hoping for heaven but headed for hell.

People, not three little pigs. People, not princes and princesses. People, not products of the imagination. People.

You, me and five-and-a-half billion others.

If life is a fairy tale, then many are finding themselves still stuck with the giant. They've been running scared so long they can't find their way back to the beanstalk. The big, bad wolves of the world still huff and puff and blow down humans who have opted not to buy bricks. Joyful living hopefuls welcome themselves into houses that seem sweet, only to find witches waiting on the inside. People who turn their life's pages daily but have yet to come to the part where the witch falls in the oven or the giant falls off the vine. Still on the lookout for one house with a chimney but finding only fellow straw-enthusiasts.

If you have bitten into the shiny apple that looked promising but was packed with poison, this book is for you. For all those tired of waiting for your prince to come, welcome to hope. Life in the real world with real possibilities for a fairytale finish.

Here is hope for all whose god is less than spectacular and only slightly more than ordinary. Come fly away to a world without veils. Above the clouds of confusion that have rained on your parade. The parade of joy, new purpose and fresh outlook.

Hope for all of you who have decided to put away your noisemakers and party favors for now. The tambourines were bought but the only thing shaken was your faith.

Hope for all of you whose mind is flooded with doubtful and disconcerting thoughts that continually drain you.

"Can 'He cares' be credible when my cares seem incredible?"

"Do my pictures have a place on God's heavenly refrigerator?"

"Does God love me?"

"Does he really care?"

"Can my life change?"

"Can I make a difference?"

"Is 'life to the full' only for fools?"

"Should I try again?"

Bring back the floats, strike up the marching band and don't bother with the umbrella. The sun is out and so is God. Grab your lawn chair, get a friend and watch God go by. He will *ooh* you, *aah* you and altogether amaze you. He will send you home happy you came. A parade of lights that will turn yours on. Introducing God.

God is, and has always been, a show-stopper. But what comes to mind when you think of God? That question has compelled me to write this book. Even greater, the answers to that question have compelled me to write this book. Too many different answers. Not enough answers. "I don't know" answers. "I'm not sure" answers. "Haven't thought much about it" answers.

There are answers. Right answers. Correct concepts. Truth. Guesses about God must go. Multiple-choice mania must become obsolete. There is a God and he can be known. For much of my life, however, veils hung in my spiritual closet. I wore one daily. The truth of God was veiled. I did not see him. I needed an unveiling. Many still do.

What is the problem? Why are so many eyelids shut to the God who opened them? Could it be Satan? The church lady jokes about him on Saturday Night Live episodes, and he jokes about church ladies attending dead services on Sunday morning. Demonic laughter. *Haha*s from hell. Riddles ripping religion. Punchlines about pew space. Hear the laughter? Listen closely.

Mom and Dad argue about which church they will attend today, his or hers. *Ha Ha!*

The teenager falls asleep during the point on peer pressure. *Giggle, giggle.*

The once full-of-life church-goer opens not the Bible but a worship manual, methodically echoing the stained glass voice from the pulpit he has heard for more than 40 years. *Ha Ha!*

The newlyweds arrive for 10:00 a.m. service longing for relatability but looking only at gray heads. *Giggle, giggle.*

The eight-year-old boy is dropped off at church by his

parents. They want Junior to learn about God but themselves have reserved no time for him this Sunday. Hard to hang when you're hung over. *Ha Ha!*

The laughter intensifies. Gut-splitting.

Demons of division flaunt copies of the yellow-pages church section. Demons of tradition distribute copies of creedbooks to fellow truth-haters. Excuse demons report the number of no-shows to their master. Demons of false security display a computerized printout of names in the billions, souls lost in God's book, saved in theirs. The demons are cutting up. All hell breaks loose.

A new shipment of veils has just arrived. Veil showrooms are once again abuzz and veil sales are at an all-time high. God-deserters looking for a piece of the action hone in on unsuspecting buyers. Aggressive angels gone astray. Once-willing servants of Deity, now merely pawns of the devil. Full-time employees of the evil one, hired to send you and me to hell.

And the spiritual battle rages. Most have no clue as to the intensity of this battle. The battle for the veil. Most are unassuming and unprepared. No camouflage. No shield. No weapons. Just a hurting heart wearing a big bull's-eye ready to be struck by bazookas from below. Bazookas loaded with veil-shaped ammunition accurately aimed right between billions of wide-open but empty eyes.

Satan loves veils. The veil covering God. The veil covering human's hearts. He has a corner on the market. All colors. All shapes. All sizes. Veils that blind mankind, leading to fear and folly. Veils that usher in spiritual fog—wrecking lives, dashing hopes and emptying lives that could be full. Cheap veils! More than likely, *you will be paid* for your purchase. Satan is not in it for the money but to make you love money, or love anything more than the Creator.

But this is not a book about Satan. No great attempt will be made here to uncover secrets of the enemy. Let's look at the friend. Let's uncover God. The real God. Let's start the unveiling process. Put aside preconceived notions and put on some glory glasses. Take off the veil that Satan has given you. I think you will like what you see.

The concept is simple. Wrap a filet-mignon and salivating ceases. It could be a filet-o-fish. Watched a child open a present lately? Absolutely no regard for the wrapping paper. Demolition derby in diapers. Give me what is on the inside. Uncover. Unwrap. Unveil.

Maybe you have been playing spiritual "Let's Make A Deal," guessing which door or curtain God might be behind. Oh no, you did it again! You picked the consolation prize. You got the dud god. If you have been a regular contestant and keep coming away with a dud, here is an opportunity to trade it in for the big deal of the day. Remember the few times when the lady in the clown suit won some bozo prize like King Kong's rocking chair in the preliminaries, but because other contestants were unwilling to part with their LA-Z-BOY recliners and console televisions for a chance at the Big Deal, Clara the Clown gladly accepted the offer and went from reject to Rio de Janeiro. How about it? Willing to go for it?

A few comments before we move on. This book has serious limitations.

I am a sinful, dying human trying to teach you about a perfect, eternal God.

I took science classes. God made Albert Einstein.

I play basketball. God made Michael Jordan.

I draw pictures (usually poor stick men). God spoke the universe into existence.

I use a telescope. God placed the stars.

I fill the bathtub. God flooded the world.

You get the point. I am on a different plane. More appropriately, God is on a different plane. He pilots the Concorde while we ride in the baggage compartment of a Cessna. Nevertheless, it is and has always been God's plan to use humans to teach humans about himself. Here is simply what one human has discovered about his Creator.

As you read, understand that the armed forces of evil

march with purpose and passion. With sophisticated weaponry, they continually assault their enemy, God. The battlefield? Your heart, your mind. Their leader? Lucifer. Your
chances? Slim, if you're not prepared.

Destined for eternal destruction, knowing and hating it,
Satan rallies his troops. He is the self-appointed leader of
the losers. The first to turn his back on the Almighty. With
no hope of heaven and their home base hell, the devil and
his demons angrily roam the earth, taking full advantage of
the loosing allowed by their former commander. A victory
for them is simple. Do not let humans see God. Provide the
trap. Prepare the veil. Glue the veil. They battle the armed
forces of good.

Jehovah's messengers. A victory for them is simple. Proclaim the truth. Grab the veil. Burn the veil. The determin-
ing factor—you! Your mind, your heart, your prayers, your
decisions.

Judgment day will unveil the winners and losers. Demonic
laughter will turn to wailing. Angels and humans who sur-
rendered to veil salesmen will gasp for relief but find none.
*Haha*s from hell will halt. Giggles gone. Riddles removed.
Punchlines packed away. Church yellow pages, no-show ros-
ters, and creedbooks will be only embers from the fires that
will scorch every resident of hell. Satan will no longer lead
and lie, but go out to an everlasting destruction for his hei-
nous war crimes. Only those who refuse Beelzebub's brain-
washing will escape the torment. Those whose hearts are set
on believing in, then following the true God will enjoy the
last laugh. *Haha*s from heaven. The mere beginnings of
praise.

Ha- Ha- Hallelujah. Ha- Ha- Hallelujah.

Then all heaven will break loose in exaltation and jubilation. Angels will raise and wave copies of battle plans for
your soul that proved successful.

Hallelujah! Hallelujah!

Your best friend will reveal the pages from his Bible that
kept him from giving in and giving up.

Hallelujah! Hallelujah!

All the redeemed will watch with thankful hearts and tearless eyes as the Son of God raises his arms in triumph, exposing the nail marks that changed their lives.

Hallelujah! Hallelujah!

And you, yes you, will join in the jubilation, sensing the overwhelming presence of your invisible God, seeing the unquestionable love in the eyes of your Savior, and walking hand-in-hand with that one special person who helped you most to make it. And for all eternity you will rejoice in your decision to be a part of the unveiling.

May this book help you in some way to participate in that much-anticipated reunion. May it give you direction to the beanstalk, access to life's destruction-proof building materials and a plan to overcome the enemy and find your way to the Father.

Chapter Two

The Blasphemy

*"You who say that people should not commit adultery,
do you commit adultery? You who abhor idols, do you rob
temples? You who brag about the law, do you dishonor
God by breaking the law? As it is written: 'God's name is
blasphemed among the Gentiles because of you'"
(Romans 2:22-24).*

arsh. Distant. Rude. Unrelatable. Cruel. Uncaring. Angry. Overbearing. Murderer. Unfair. Difficult. Cynical. Unloving. Mean. Intense. Weird. Insincere. Unfriendly. Schizophrenic. Thief. Confusing. Stupid. Terrible. Demented. Unsympathetic.

Sounds like a composite of any one of those 10 individuals you may recognize from your last post-office visit. The worst of the worst. The avoid-at-all-cost people. The frightening ones you pray to never meet in a dark alley—sure to strike fear into even the best-trained blackbelt.

"This person really needs God."

Sad to say, but in the minds of many, this *describes* God. Could God be the bad guy? Is he a prime candidate for post-office photography? Could the Creator be criminal?

For those presently struggling to believe in God's "good-guy" status, basic day-to-day life can become a confusing and continual battle. A nightmare without end. They're living in a hateful, dog-eat-dog world, trying desperately to hang on and make a mark, but with only bite marks to show for it.

Oh, most of these doubters have heard of a good God. They probably even at one time believed in a good God. Mom and Dad made sure. But something went wrong. They no longer believe, or they believe no longer than a few minutes, a day, a week, or until that one special "relationship to end all relationships" does just that—ends. Hope has faded. Survival is now the key.

This book is dedicated to all who need a fresh perspective of God. For all who have lost touch with reality. For any looking to be paroled from the prison of poor perception. Now, before you start thinking of all those "who could really use this book," take a moment, a few days, a week (however long it takes you to read 203 pages) and see if it is not *you* who really needs this. I know I do. I need help—lots of it. Every day I need God. The real God. The only God.

Blasphemous accusations about God have been around a long time, beginning with the "God is so selfish he doesn't want you to know what he knows" lie that ended in paradise lost. The first couple who got bit by the slithery serpent and soon after bit into the fruit of failure.

"Oh, no, we're naked!."

"Oops."

Work. Sweat. Thorns. Thistles. Labor pains. Submission.

Satan had succeeded with his blasphemous efforts, and in all the years since the disastrous deception in the garden, believing the blasphemy has continued to be man's major mistake.

And Satan loves to capitalize.

His well-organized business meetings are still complete with blasphemous agendas. Demons directed to lie, cheat and swindle for a profit—one soul lost for eternity. Frenzied fireside chats where blueprints of blasphemy are developed to slander the name of the Lord and lessen your chances of survival.

"If we can make God less spectacular, he will become more optional."

"All in favor say 'Aye.'" Hell explodes.
"All opposed?" Silence.
"Meeting adjourned."
I can already hear some of you lying to yourself:
"Me? Not me! Oh, no, I'm a Christian."
"I have never thought those things."
"I couldn't. That wouldn't be right."
"I could go to hell if I think that about God."
"Perish the thought."
But the *thought* will not cause you to perish. Denial might.
Join me for a minute. Been down these roads before?
Heard these voices? Thought these thoughts? I call them
my "Bottom 25." They're in no particular order, but all of
them are ugly. First the thought. Then the translation.

1) "The Christian life is too challenging with not enough
   help to make it."
   God is harsh.
2) "God, why aren't you listening? Do you hear me? I do
   not feel close to you, God."
   God is distant.
3) "God, couldn't you say that in a more encouraging way?"
   God is rude.
4) "Easy for you to say, God. You have no problems."
   God is unrelatable.
5) "God, you like watching me suffer, don't you?"
   God is cruel.
6) "There are five billion people in the world. Who am I
   anyway?"
   God is uncaring.
7) "I just know God loves to punish me."
   God is angry.
8) "God, I just went over my limit; I need a break."
   God is overbearing.
9) "God why did you take my baby, my mom, my brother,
   my best friend, my wife?"
   God is a murderer.

10) "God, I am living much better than they are. Why am I going through this and not them?"
    God is unfair.

11) "God, I don't understand the Bible. Couldn't you have said it in fewer words?"
    God is difficult.

12) "God, you just made hell to hurt us. Sure, you don't have to worry about it."
    God is cynical.

13) "Why don't I have more friends, God? Why do I always go everywhere alone?"
    God is unloving.

14) "She is so nice. Why did you let that happen to her?"
    God is mean.

15) "All these commands, God, and so little time to obey them."
    God is too intense.

16) "What is this 'first shall be last, last first; lose you get, and get you lose' lingo?"
    God is weird.

17) "You say you love me, God, but I'm really not feeling it."
    God is insincere.

18) "Why aren't you there when I need you God? You don't have time for me."
    God is unfriendly.

19) "Now, am I supposed to turn my cheek, or tell them they're going to hell?"
    God is schizophrenic.

20) "God, I have to give up what?"
    God is a thief.

21) "I still don't understand God."
    God is confusing.

22) "Why is that in the Bible?"
    God is stupid.

23) "I am just a pawn in God's heavenly chess game."
    God is terrible.

24) "Hell is not a just punishment."
    God is demented.
25) "I wish God knew what life was like having somebody
    tell you what to do all the time."
    God is unsympathetic.

This blasphemous thinking that lowers God to levels of humanistic weakness and sin rapidly swims through our bloodstream and into our hearts. We bring a "great" God down to our "normal" level and wave the devil and his interpretations into our blameshifting hearts.

Similar forms of blasphemy, propagated by so-called "believers" in the first century, allowed the skeptical and non-religious Gentiles to excuse themselves from believing in and committing to God (Romans 2:17-24). Sadder, it kept the Gentile sinners from the full life. It kept them from answers to their emptiness questions. It kept them trapped in the short-lived pleasures of frequent orgies and the long-lasting pain of divorce, drinking problems and problem children. Confusion reigned with religious chaos at the top of the charts. Where was God? Who was God? Why were God's so-called spokesmen involved in the unspeakable?

Two thousand years of open-forum preaching and Bible availability has done little to erase the problem. What is the root? Let's get to the bottom of this. Can we dig our way out? How do we get suckered into believing that God is responsible for this huge mess? We know it's not true. Or do we? Where do we learn these things? Here are some possible explanations. See if they fit in your life.

Mom and Dad tried hard but fell short. I know because I am now failing at some of those things I said "I will never do when I become a parent." Maybe you didn't have both. Maybe Dad never came home. Or when he did, alcohol came with him, in his body and in a bag. Maybe Mom's soaps superseded your afterschool specials. Maybe Dad didn't come to your games or the ones he did, you heard about the missed shots and not the great pass. Maybe Mom worked overtime to get the bike you wanted, but you never got to tell her about the times you got your feelings hurt at school. Maybe Dad didn't know how to say "I love you." Maybe you had all the possessions, but now you would give all you possess for one good talk with your parents. Or maybe report cards brought home were analyzed, scrutinized and sterilized. A 'B' from Mr. Smith in Algebra was an 'F' with Dad. A 'C' in World Civilization was uncivilized.

"I tried, Mom."

"It comes really hard for me."

"I did my best."

These phrases, however true, were never taken into consideration. Nor were the angelic whispers to Mom and Dad's conscience to "Take time to ask about algebra" or "Turn off the television and help her with her homework."

Family meals were like memorials spent in moments of silence. Others were akin to police interrogations. No wonder seats remain plentiful at the banquet table with God. Vacations were an opportunity to see family friction at dangerous levels. If heaven is an eternal vacation, we would rather stay home.

Spankings? What are they? No spankings and no discipline mean little or no respect for God. God is loose, and so are you.

Spankings? No response, just tears. Too many spankings and now you resist the outstretched hand of God for fear it harms, not heals. Your backside had regular board meetings, but hugs, explanations and prayers were not on the agenda.

Maybe Mom hurt you. Maybe Dad. Maybe you still don't know. Maybe you don't want to know. Maybe it was emotional abuse that left you afraid to feel. Or the continual "Shut-up!"'s that now have you shut down. Perhaps it was physical abuse that left you wearing long sleeves in the summer and left you at the short end of the stick year-round.

Our parents taught us a lot about God. Whether you had a "747" Jumbo Bible on your living room coffee table or the first Bible you read was to your children, Mom and Dad were constantly—and mostly unknowingly—leaving us with "God-impressions."

Mom and Dad represent just two of the individuals in our lives who play the "horrible" role of *the authority*. There are many more. Our lives are surrounded by authority. The perceived bad guys. The "get in line" guys. The "stop it do this do that" guys. The ones we answer to. The coach. The teacher. The boss. The police. The President. The government. The professor.

So what is your impression? Believe it or not, one bad experience with any of these authorities can leave a bad and lasting taste that sours you toward God. I've had good and bad authorities. Often I did not know at the time which was which, but now I do. I will spare the details to spare the guilty, but suffice it to say, I am ecstatic that the one in charge of my eternal destiny differs drastically from former mentors.

How about you? Relate?

The boss who supplied the paychecks but not the pleasantries.

The teacher who gave you awful marks but had no office hours.

The coach who chewed you out but never chewed the fat.

The government official who wanted your vote but not your phone call.

And the list goes on.

I am not saying authority is bad. On the contrary, God gives us authority and expects us to completely submit (Romans 13:1-6, 1 Peter 2:13-18). Nevertheless, some have allowed these ungodly, semi-godly, or somewhat godly authorities to keep them from pursuing and then loving their ultimate authority, God.

Wish we could stop there. But some of the most powerful mediums of blasphemy remain. Religious hypocrisy is one we all have probably experienced, either through seeing it or being it, undoubtedly a little of both. This form of blasphemy can bring on any of the following statements:

"Well, if God is like that, I want nothing to do with him."

"They are still the same as they were when they got religious."

"I thought he said he followed God."

"They're just a bunch of hypocrites."

"If I follow God, I can't really have any fun."

"If Christianity is the only way, why are there about 500 versions?"

"Just turning on the TV turns me off to God."

Worship services that leave people wanting—but not wanting God. Come in late, leave early.

"Come again when you can," the minister says with a smile, shaking the hand of an irregular attendee.

"Hope you can make it next week."

Robes, choirs and committees without righteousness, challenges or commitment. Evangelism is attempted by a few but shunned by the majority. Members' money goes into building ministers' mansions.

Black churches. White churches. Suburban churches. Inner-city churches.

Bible most. Bible some. Bible no.

Church bulletins being read more often than the Bible. Christmas church extravaganzas attended by the thousands, early morning prayer sessions by the tens.

And this is where God lives? God is in this church? No wonder people don't come. This is it folks. Wish it were better news.

Should I continue? The guy at work with enough Jesus, God and Bible paraphernalia to cover his car, your car and the Good Year Blimp. He *must* be full of nothing but hot air because he continually gives the cold shoulder.

The crosses that hang from the necks of non-virgins. The cross doesn't help to keep her clothes on when "Mr. Seems Right" offers his empty promises. Nor does it remind him of the One who died to forgive him of and keep him from what he is about to do.

Creedbooks being studied, memorized, honored and heralded more than Christ's books. Doctrine that plays second fiddle to comfort and tradition.

"Holy Wars Escalate"
Isn't that a contradiction in terms?
"Religious Leader Guilty of Child Molestation"
Whatever happened to leading by example?
"Send me $50, and I'll send you my prayer towel."
Since when did prayer have a price tag?
Looked at the religion page in your newspaper lately? In many American cities its headline reads, **"Visit the Church of Your Choice."** Sounds like Baskin-Robbins and the Bible!
"Divorce Rates Increasing Among Church-Goers"
If God can't help my marriage, what else matters?

No wonder people have a hard time with God. Religion has often damaged God's reputation more than upheld it. A big, messy situation requiring a Godzilla-sized paper towel.

The media has also aided in the blasphemy of God. Unfortunately, there are not many God-lovers in the field, but plenty of story-searchers, looking for the big break. Consequently, sensationalism and lies persist in the media.

How much can we or should we trust of what we read in the newspaper or hear on the news? Is "Headline News" all true? How do you know? Is the front-page as up-front as we assume?

I remember a conversation with a neighbor in San Diego seven years ago that opened my eyes to what I call "media manipulation."

The church I was a minister with in San Diego had received some persecution via the airwaves and printing presses, and I thought my neighbor might have seen it. I was curious to find out for sure, so I asked if he had seen the newscasts or read the papers. He said he had not but added that he would not have believed it anyway. As a fireman, he indicated he would often come home from fighting a fire and see the local news account and think it was a different fire altogether. Translation: the media was televising the "incredible five-alarm blaze that threatened mankind's existence" while he was fighting the two-alarm blaze that did an estimated $15,000 damage. And they can get away with it. Unfortunately we often believe what we hear.

I wonder how many lies about God, his nature and his followers have been spread over the years through the ink and influence of the media?

Editorials that have enabled Satan to speak his piece.

Columnists consistently destroying the pillars of truth.

Editors more committed to the deadline than the bottom line.

The dangers of radical religion regularly find front-page privileges with the likes of Jim Jones and David Koresh, making most readers suspicious at best about anything radical.

But wasn't Jesus radical? And didn't he command those considering the option of wearing his name to be just like him (1 John 2:5-6)?

All the while, truth-seekers and good-deed-doers, when allowed in, are sent to the back of the bus called "Blasphemy" in the papers of prejudice.

The last blasphemer we look at will undoubtedly be the most painful. It's you. It's me.

"A man's own folly ruins his life, yet his heart rages against the Lord" (Proverbs 19:3).

Is that not true? We get mad at God because it is too painful to admit we blew it. How many times have you blamed God for your own blunders?

How about your marriage problems?

"God, if you had just led me to someone who was more like me, we would not have all these problems."

Your children?

"God, why can't you just make them obey?!"

Your money problems?

"God, I have been praying for months for a raise, and you still haven't answered."

The real problem? You haven't had a date with your wife in two years and she hasn't had the pleasure of seeing a flower-delivery man since your last anniversary.

The real problem? You haven't disciplined your children consistently. They take advantage of you and then become afraid of you because when you finally get involved, you become the Mt. St. Helens of motherhood.

The real problem? You haven't kept a budget for six months and never balance your checkbook. You thought about cutting up the credit cards but couldn't find the scissors right then.

Let's admit it. *We* are the problem, not God.

The positive HIV tests results.

"It was the Lord, not my lifestyle."

The break-up.

"My girlfriend left me, and God took away the only girl I ever loved."

Or did the lust, lies and lack of getting guidance cause her to finally see the chinks in your armor?

The second letter from the university informing you that your scholarship money would not be coming anymore due to "unsatisfactory performance." Was it God? Or was it girls? Was it the Almighty? Or was it the alcohol? Was it the Lord? Or was it the late nights?

"It was the wife you gave me."

"It was the kids you gave me."

"It was the job you gave me."

"It was the in-laws you gave me."

And then it becomes "the wife you didn't give me;" "the kids you didn't give me;" and "the job you didn't give me." I'm glad I am not God. Lightning rods would be in high demand.

The blasphemy. The contributors—parents, all authority figures, religious hypocrisy, the media and me.

But don't believe the lies. Don't give Satan any more success stories to share by the fire.

Chapter Three

The Search

"My son, if you accept my words, and store up my
commands within you, turning your ear to wisdom and
applying your heart to understanding, and if you call out
for insight and cry aloud for understanding,
and if you look for it as silver and search for it as hidden
treasure, then you will understand the fear of the Lord
and find the knowledge of God"
(Proverbs 2:1-5).

Whether it is looking for the keys, our kids, or a cloud's silver lining, much of our lives are spent searching. We need. We search. Usually, we find. We will swim through trash to find a lost letter, a misplaced phone number, even an overdue bill. Man will go ape looking for the missing link without checking God's chain of events. Humans go crazy searching for answers and stay crazy because God is out of the question.

Why don't more people search for God in the same way? Weighted veils.

But you *can* know God. You can find God. You can understand him and find gems from the generous One. There are answers to life's problems, cares and concerns and directions to the pearly gates of the eternal Promised Land.

So where do you begin? You must begin with a vow. A promise to yourself that you will not stop looking until you

find. Let's drift back to our days of youth and take a re-
fresher course in hide-and-seek...

First, you decide to play. (You can't overlook the obvious.)

Second, you must select an "It."

"It" closes his eyes (all the way) and participants bolt off
to sophisticated hiding places.

"It" counts to 100 (all the way), opens his eyes (this will
come in handy later), and begins his midget manhunt.

"It" locates all the hidden—game over.

Choose another "It" and continue.

It is time for the adult version that will put the kid back
in all of us.

Deciding to play hide-and-seek was at times a tough decision. What about all the options? What about capture the
flag? Why not baseball? Marbles? Let's stay inside and play
video games. Monopoly?

The decision to search for God can be tough also. What
about my job? Is there time? Do I really feel like it? Isn't
there something else to do? Isn't it good enough that I believe in him? Right now school is cramping my style. Searching for God may just crush me. And if I search I may not
have time for recreation, sports, or any other fun activities.
And besides, how will this search affect my budget?

So many options to the Omnipotent One. But you must
be aware that if you are going to find God you must *search* for
him.

"When I finish high school I will."

Liar!

"When the pace slows down at work we definitely will
talk about it."

Liar!

"When I get done with my finals, I cross my heart, hope
to die promise I will come to church."

You say it: Liar!

"When I find some free time, I will study the Bible."

"When I get married, my wife and I together will look for
a church."

"When we start a family, I definitely want my kids to learn about God."

This illness, that situation, this trial, that trouble. That's baloney! Ninety-nine percent of the time people don't follow through on these "When..." promises. They never get around to it. So much is happening. So much pleasure to ponder. Oodles to obtain. Besides, what will I find if I search for God? Will it be good? Will it be fun? Will it be worthwhile? Deciding is a big deal.

Guess who's "It"? As much as we would like it to be, "It" is not God. That leaves you and me. God has always been looking for a relationship with us. He has been "It" for eternity, so it's about time we took a turn.

Oh sure, we've played the game, but all we ever do is hide. We hide from our problems. From our fears. From our sins. From our God. We have hopped aboard Jonah's cruiseliner. We sleep in the bottom and hide from reality. We recreate at poolside and ignore the fact that our life is taking a dive. We admire at the observation deck, trying to convince ourselves that life is peaceful and painless. We talk shop with other ticket-holders all the while avoiding the inevitable—a big appointment with a big fish.

The whales are still alive. (A whale is the biggest fish I know of, but if Jonah lived in a shark for three days, God is even more incredible.) Hungry whales. Wide-mouth whales. You have probably been in one and did not even notice.

The death of a close friend and fellow partier.

A firing.

A ruined relationship that still rubs you.

A night of pillow tears.

A divorce.

A brush with death that brushed you back.

A 'D'.

An 'F'.

A jail sentence.

A fit of rage which led to that "something" you said you would never do.

The whales are everywhere. God's swallowing servants setting you up for some time alone. Are you in a whale? Don't fret, you're still alive. But get out of there. It is dark, clammy and downright disgusting. You could be doing much better. Take a few minutes and read the book of Jonah. My guess is that modern-day whales will hurl, blow chunks or just plain puke you to freedom and a fresh start. As much as God let the whale swallow you, he is even more eager to open his mouth and bring some light and fresh air to your life. Better yet, if the storm is on the horizon and you are still on the boat, get off at the next port and run back to God. The ship stops whenever you say. Go ahead, Captain. You are "It." Stop hiding and go seeking. You will find.

Closing your eyes is next. Some necessary nap time if you plan on waking up. Some time to think, relax and focus. We are usually in such a big hurry we miss the obvious—God. Lateness led you to the fast lane of life, but you missed your exit. Slow down. Think for a minute. When was the last time you really thought about where you were headed in life? What are your goals? One week goals? One month goals? One year? Five years? Lifetime? Thought about purpose lately? "What purpose?" That may be the problem. What have you accomplished in life up till today? Important and essential questions that most will never ask. Sure it may hurt to hear the truth, but see if it doesn't help.

Relax for a minute. Life's precious moments are passing you by, leaving you looking at the smoke and exhausted. You may have just missed one. One becomes two. Two becomes four. Four becomes 10. Ten becomes 100. How many have you missed? Don't miss them! If you do, you may miss God.

Now some of you are enjoying this point too much. You majored in relaxation in college and now your diploma hangs over your couch and your stomach. "Relax" does not mean recline in the seat of life. But most of us really need this. You may be neurotic, you just haven't been diagnosed. You could be a controlled schizophrenic. But you really don't need the couch, you just need to calm down. Slow down and catch the exit. Just make sure it's God's exit.

Pray for a while. I did not say a minute. While one minute with God can be both powerful and productive, it will never adequately equip us for life, nor does it lend honor to an ever-present, always-hearing God. Do you pray? How much? Does it help? You will not find God unless you decide to start praying.

So now you are convicted and convinced. You and God have an early-morning date. The alarm is set for 6:00 a.m.

Actual time to arise is 6:56 a.m.—or eight angry slaps of the snooze alarm.

Time to go for a walk or take the car to the park. You have to get away. Jesus did, and you are going to be just like Jesus.

Actual course of events—plop on couch, assume fetal position, pull blanket over your head, begin to pray, pray until 7:01 (you don't know exactly).

Wake up at 7:45 in spiritual fog.

Rush into the shower.

Quickly inhale half a bowl of stale cereal.

Rush out the door, drive to work and the day you hoped would be different already has begun in an all-too-familiar fashion. You try to convince yourself you prayed a powerful 45 minutes and then slept for 10, but you know better.

No wonder we struggle. No wonder we don't feel God. It is time to get tough with your time with God. Nobody butts in. Nothing comes before it. You protect that time like the Secret Service protects their president. Get some conviction. Get up. Get out. Get into it. Get on with your life. You can't really search unless you really pray.

Focus for a while. All the time would be best. Do you focus? What is your focus? What is in the center ring of your circus? Typically, if you take time to think, relax and pray you will be focused. So close your eyes (but don't sleep!). You will be amazed how open they will get.

Now for the good part. In hide-and-seek, players pick inconspicuous and inconceivable locations in which to lay low. Holes, closets, bushes—our choices of camouflage. Good news. God is not hiding in a hole. He fills even the universe. He's not hiding in a locked closet. Every door available is ajar. He's not behind a bush, or if he is, it's probably burning. Ask Moses. God is in obvious hiding places. He *wants* you to find him. He makes weird noises so you will walk in his direction. He throws objects your way to draw your attention to him. He does everything except find himself for you.

Yet even with all the helpful hints, we often respond with, "I can't do it" or "It's too hard" or "I tried once and it didn't help. Could you do it for me?" Sounds like my five-year-old. If only we would *try*. If only we went about it in the right way, with sincerity and tenacity. God is there. He is everywhere. And he loves being found.

Counting to 100 was always a challenge for me as a kid. But those were the rules. It gave you time to think. "Now where would Joey hide? Would Jennifer go to the barn or the backyard? What are their options? Where could they be?" The count slowed you down. The adrenaline was so high you welcomed the deep breaths. You can already see the analogy. So many want God and go after God but don't use what God gave them—their brains. Take a breather. Think. Where would God go? Where will I go first to find him? Second? Third? Think. Think some more. Think again. (Save some of the emotion for when you find him.) For now, climb down from your scarecrow's post, stuff yourself with some wisdom and start using your brain.

Now you can open your eyes. Sounds obvious, but how successful could you be in hide-and-seek if you never opened your eyes? Open your eyes and see the signs of God. Open your eyes to the creation. It speaks of a powerful, yet orderly Creator. When was the last time you gazed at the stars for more than a minute? When was the last time you saw a sunset—intentionally? Get to a park, a beach or a mountain, and see God. Whether you live in Bellingham, Washington; Portland, Oregon; San Diego, California; Denver, Colorado; Lincoln, Nebraska; Cincinnati, Ohio; or Chicago, Illinois; (my resting places the past 15 years) all you have to do is open your eyes.

The rain. The tide. The Columbia River. The Ohio River. Lake Michigan. The Pacific. The Plains. The greens. The reds. The browns. The golds. The snow. The Cascades. The rocks. The Rockies.

Go take a walk. Take a hike. Buy a train ticket. Board the bus. Get on a plane. Do whatever necessary, but make sure when you're there, you open your eyes.

Open your eyes to the Bible. God introduces himself to you and you to truth.

"Peek-a-boo, here I am."

"Over here."

"Wait, no, you're going the wrong way."

"Getting warmer, warmer."

"Cold, colder."

Thud!! The sound of a dropped Bible.

Slam!! The cover shuts.

You stopped reading. Only one more page and you were there. You still possess a copy but think you will need to be possessed before you read it again. But if you want to find God, you will need to pick it up again and resume reading. Scribes spent sleepless nights writing down each letter carefully so we could know God. Dotting each "i" and crossing each "t." Spend some late nights reading, so their late nights won't have been in vain.

Open your eyes to people. Though, granted, they are the main contributors to blasphemy, God still uses people to aid your search. People who love God. Non-hypocrites. Not perfect, but working on perfecting.

"Fresh air. Can it be? Can others actually help me to find God?"

Yes, in fact, you cannot find God without them. God has always used others to act as guides for the blind. Eyes to point us in the proper direction. To set us on a straight course. Even Paul, who saw Jesus on the road to Damascus, needed extra eyes, and God used Ananias to bring sight to the blind

Pharisee (Acts 22:1-16). We all need extra eyes. God used the eyes of Patty, Bob, Preston, Kenny, George, Gregg, Gordon, Mike, Drew, Jay, Ron (at least two of them), John (at least three of them) and others to help me see. Suddenly, the usually insulting "four eyes" has new and positive connotations. God will give you at least four if you are willing. But the more, the better.

Open your eyes to your need. God set eternity in your heart and now you're settling for 70, maybe 80 years? You need something. You are living with a gigantic cavity in your heart that pains you daily. God longs to fill it. Just get yourself an appointment. Stop trying to fill it with your job, your spouse, your family, money, drugs, recreation, sex or power and start relying upon God.

Need purpose? God fills you with the dream of bringing others to him.

Need people? God has some special selections that will fill you with joy.

Need principle? God has a book that will fill you with truth.

Need problems solved? God has a plan to fill the gaps.

Ready to search? Go back and read Proverbs 2:1-5 again. Did you see that? Wow!! It's a done deal! Look out Las Vegas! This is a winner every time. No risk involved—just effort. The 'E' word. 'E' for eliminate. Billions of souls eliminated from solid salvation possibilities simply because they are not willing to make the effort. Don't let it be said of you.

Now, let me get this straight. If I do verses one through four, I get verse five automatically? Read it one more time. Two letters never packed a bigger punch—'I-F'. If. A conditional word. You do your part; God does his. A covenant. An agreement. God has conducted business this way since sounding the starting gun. Adam and Eve, Noah, Abraham, Moses, Saul, Solomon and numerous others all had to sign on the dotted line. The deals were simple.

Adam and Eve:

"No fruit, or no life."
Noah:
"Build a boat for the water, or be destroyed by the water."
Abraham:
"Pull down your pants and be cut, or be cut off."
Moses:
"Talk to the rock, or you will only talk about the Promised Land."
Saul:
"Destroy all the Amalekites, or I will destroy your leadership."
Solomon:
"Take no foreign women, or foreign men will take you."
Some succeeded. Some failed. But all had an "If." So do we.

"... if you accept my words..."

It is God's way or no way. Sounds elementary and easily achievable until you meet up with the first verse in the Bible "you've never seen before" or "were taught differently while growing up." Billions will forfeit their home in heaven because they could not get past verse one. What is it for you?

Tradition? Mom? Dad? Boyfriend? Pastor? Feelings? Fear?

Get some guts, and do what you are told.

"... store up my commands..."

Humble yourself a minute, and sit at the feet of a chipmunk. Storing up is basic to survival for "Chip" and his animal kingdom friends. Whether it's snow for the squirrels, a blizzard for the birds, or just Satan's surprise attacks, life necessitates having some "on hand" supplies. It's beyond reading the Bible. It's memorizing. Storing up. Putting the commands away in your heart to use when you need them most.

"... turning your ear to wisdom..."

Becoming experts at eavesdropping on heavenly conversations.

"Did you hear what God told Job?"

"You would not believe what Jesus told the Twelve about kids and the kingdom."

"Now exactly what did God tell Moses about cancelling his Promised Land reservations?"

"Did you catch that stuff in Revelation about revival?"

Wisdom is waiting to enter your ears. Go ahead. Scoot over and listen up.

"... apply your heart to understanding..."

Not your head, your heart. Gear up! Get your emotions out of neutral and start *feeling* again. You need God, but you can't have him until you offer him your heart. Your heart may be heavy, but you are not a spiritual Tin Man. Granted, some effort may be required to get it beating right again, but it is in there. Fighting to be heard. Wanting to hurt. Needing to feel. Looking to have a good laugh one more time. Hoping for a good cry. Wanting to be excited about God. Hoping you will realize that it is okay to tell the whole truth about your whole life. That it is even acceptable to express frustration and anger.

Certainly, hearts were not meant to be broken, but neither were they meant to remain silent. Oil the chambers of your heart, oh Tin Man, and start sharing. God loves to see your heart. Then the good news: He will change it!

"... and if you call out for insight..."

If your plane has crashed and rescue seems only remotely possible, grab the biggest stick you can find and start writing your SOS. Don't stick with those stupidity statements bound for the "I Can't Believe I Said That" Hall of Fame, like:

"Oh, I'll be all right."

"I can handle this alone."

"I really don't need anybody."

"It's really not all that bad."

Bite your lip next time. Draw blood if you need to. Get humble, and you will hear the heavenly helicopter on the horizon. Your soul is just about saved.

"... and cry aloud for understanding..."

Sounds desperate. It is. Then why is the pillow your best

pal. Have you talked to God about it? Are others invited to your pain party? Turn up the volume on your tears. God will never turn them down.

"... and if you look for it as for silver and search for it as for hidden treasure..."

Where the rubber meets the road. What separates the men from the boys. Where the line is being drawn. Overused cliches that are seldom taken seriously. People not willing to work at it or for it. Inviting God over for dinner and expecting him to bring the food. And clean up. And provide the entertainment. Invitation declined!

God looks to spend time with men and women willing to take responsibility. To do the digging and find the gold. Determined. Daring. Dreamers. God looks for people like the 49ers. Men and women with guts and a goal and a work ethic. Willing to sacrifice family, comfort and security for something greater, fueled by an insatiable desire to find wealth. Hidden wealth. They came from near and far to California. In their wagons. On their horses. Some died on the way. Others died there. Some found. Some did not. Some got rich. Others got nothing. But all had character. The insides of champions. You don't name a football team after ordinary people. And you don't find God without character.

Looked for treasure lately? Gone after any gold? Most of us have had our treasures handed to us. We have worked very little for what we have. The 49ers to us are football players, not fanatics. Nevertheless, their drive for the treasure is much like the example God chose to show us what it will take to find the truth. We must be gold diggers to walk the golden streets. You want your mansion? Start building. Expecting a joyful eternity? Exert the effort.

Now for the scary part. Take away just one "if" and your chances are less than "iffy." Accepting the Bible without accepting the help is unacceptable. Searching for treasure without a plan for the pearls will only bring temporary joy. You find 'em. You lose 'em.

Now for the exciting part. We can sign on to every "if."
God *has* never and *will* never command the impossible (1
John 5:3). God has set you up for success. You *can* understand. You *can* find. There is treasure available. Go ahead,
grab a nugget. There is gold enough for everybody.

Chapter Four

The Purpose

> *"Now we know that if the earthly tent we live in is destroyed, we have a building from God, an eternal house in heaven, not built by human hands. Meanwhile we groan, longing to be clothed with our heavenly dwelling, because when we are clothed, we will not be found naked. For while we are in this tent, we groan and are burdened, because we do not wish to be unclothed but to be clothed with our heavenly dwelling, so that what is mortal may be swallowed up by life. Now it is God who has made us for this very purpose and has given us the Spirit as a deposit, guaranteeing what is to come"*
>
> *(2 Corinthians 5:1-5).*

"So what's in it for me?"

"What will God give me for my serious search efforts?"

Selfish questions, but all of us ask them. God wants us to ask them. He loves to answer them. And the answer will be the same for each interrogator. Heaven. It is the goal. It is what life and death are all about.

For many years, the question of Why? plagued me. Why am I here? Why did God make me? I asked a few times, got no solid answers, so I stopped asking. Then I stopped caring. I wasn't alone. Maybe you were there. Maybe you are there today.

I remember a discussion in 1986 at a Sunday night Bible class in Portland, Oregon, that had potential to be a life-changer. My life-changer. The class had no real structure (that should have clued me in right there), but at the time I didn't mind too much. We were discussing having children and why and how we should decide to have more. We had a three-month-old at the time so there was some interest on my part. The topic quickly shifted to God and why he made man. We agreed that if we could determine why God made man we could answer our initial question. It looked to be a step in the right direction. Was there an answer? Maybe tonight was the night? Somebody must know. There were 20 full-grown, church-going, Bible-believers in that room. Certainly one would know. Or at least the discussion would stimulate our brains, and collectively we could conclude truth. I left that night disillusioned. Distraught. I can't blame anyone. I was there, too. Some possibilities were presented.

"Maybe he was lonely and wanted companionship."

"It is something that nobody will ever know for sure."

"He wanted us to enjoy the earth he made."

"No reason; it just happened."

Not until I read 2 Corinthians 5:1-5 did I know for sure. It became so clear. So obvious. I was made so I could go to heaven!! That is why God made all of us. He wants us to enjoy what he does. He wants to give. He wants to give me a permanent address.

Now that was an eyeball enlarger. After hearing so much about how so many will go to hell because it is so hard to get to heaven, this scripture was refreshing. God *wants* me in heaven.

Hallelujah. Honk, honk!!

That's why on some late night in August of 1958, God brought Mom and Dad together to bring me to the world. Nine months later, April 17, 1959, all nine pounds, fifteen ounces of me appeared for the first time to the general public. A fat little baby knowing nothing more than nipples and naps is destined for heaven. Your story is the same. Only the date is different. Heaven is your destiny. Welcome to the inside scoop.

Proclaim today trash day!! Time to throw away all the God-garbage smelling of wasted words like "It's too hard" or "God doesn't care about me" or "God doesn't know me" or "I'm not loved." All are destined for dump delivery.

Do you feel the veil slipping?

God wants me, Mom and the many to make it. He must, then, be doing all he can to give us the best possible chance to get there. Spiritual gas pumps are plentiful along the journey to keep us above the 'E'. Spare tires when life gets flat. Tune-ups for the tired and potentially unfulfilled pew-fillers. Alignment for the narrow road. And a perfect, easy-to-read, large-letter map to get you where you need to go. Mr. Goodwrench move over. The manufacturer, the wholesaler, the salesman and the mechanic. God does it all.

Parents who really love to spoil their children (all of us) should be hearing the bells. We want the best for our kids, don't we? It is hard for me to go to a toy store and say No. If I had the money, it's likely I would buy the store.

"Want another teenage turtle figure? Perhaps a Power Ranger or two? Okay, go ahead, take the entire display."

"A doll? Take them all!"

If God is anything like a dad taking his kids to the toy store, I would say we are set! What would God want for his children? What would you want for yours? Multiply that by about 1,000 and you are off to a slow start. How about a great education? Happiness? Health? Friends? A loving spouse? Fun? Freedom? Joy? Only the opening act of a well-rehearsed play. Heaven is the finale!

God has kids daily and an accompanying plan for each. Whether they are born in India or Indiana, Paris or Pittsburgh, God has a purpose for all of them. I can't tell you his individual plans for any of them. I can't even tell you his for me! But I don't really need to know the plan as long as I know there *is* one. There is a plan for you. It is on the Creator's computer. You are a topic of conversation in heaven.

God, Gabriel and gobs of others talk about you. Heavenly chat.

"What else can we do?"

"How can we bail her out this time?"

"What would really encourage him today?"

"How can we get them to go to church?"

"How can we humble her without humiliating her?"

"Which disciples could we put in their path today?"

"What earthly reward can we offer that will help him think of eternal treasure?"

"What must we block them from doing before they black out on God?"

"How can I convince them they are loved?"

Now that's the type of conversation about me I don't mind. Not to mention who God is setting you up to marry. Whether a boy or girl would be better for you as a parent. Which job will brighten you and not bore you. A veritable smorgasbord of activity all designed to keep you happy here and headed for the hereafter.

But let's focus, for now, on the hereafter. There are plenty of vacancies. God is leaving the light on for all of us.

A book about God would be incredibly incomplete without some information on heaven. After all, it is the purpose. It is why God made us. It is our goal. Though little of the exact nature of heaven is contained in Scripture, if God is involved and it truly is a reward for faithful living, "phenomenal" is the closest adjective I can find to describe it. Others come to mind. Awesome. Incredible. Indescribable. Fantastic. Unreal. Amazing. Wow. Wow. Yippeee.

What does the Bible say? No tears. No pain. No death. Mansions. Rooms. Golden street. Crystal Sea. Jesus. God. Angels. Joy. Love. Tree of Life. Paradise.

Sign me up. I will definitely take a room. Allow me to imagine for a moment...

One with a triple king-sized waterbed with no possibility of motion sickness and easy to get in and out of. Will I sleep on that waterbed? It doesn't matter. Personally, I am looking forward to sleeping some in heaven.

Include in my room a theater-sized television screen with mental remote. You think, you watch.

Channel 12. The apostles and what really happened. What the guys really thought when Peter was presented with the keys. The look on their faces when Jesus was a water-walker. Each one's favorite parable and why. How they handled the fame, the frantic schedule and family all at once.

Channel 2. My life and every time the angels were there to bail me out, visible this time.

Channel 3. The sports channel. Highlights of Moses and the Red Sea, in slow motion. Jonah and the fish, in 3D. Joshua and the walls of Jericho, in surround sound. Daniel in the den, the boys in the blaze and all the other best of the "you-wish-you-could-have-been-there" Bible events.

Channel 5. A review of all the right decisions you ever made. (Give yourself five.)

Channel 1. The kingdom-comes-first station. A look at all the great shows, movies and sporting events you missed on earth because your treasure was in heaven.

Channel 4. A look up-close at all the fun and crazy times you had on earth. The dates. The costume parties where nerd was normal. The roller-coaster ride with the anything-but-confident look on your face. The whitewater raft trip you said would be a piece of cake but instead ate you up. The late-night laughter with your best friends.

Channel 6. The music channel. Hear the great hymns being sung by the angelic choir. Anybody can be a member. No need to audition. We will all sing like Sinatra and Streisand.

Room-service please. I'm banking on food being there. French toast for breakfast. No worry of a bread shortage with Jesus around. Salmon for lunch (one that Peter caught), and steak for dinner (from all the fattened calves ready for a repenter but never used). And anything chocolate for desert.

Time for some reading. No room would be complete without a copy of the Bible. This will be no ordinary Bible.

A picture Bible, live-action, with an explanation of the "what in the world does that mean?" passages.

Were the six days in Genesis 24-hour days, thousands of years each, or somewhere in the middle? I'll get to watch the answer!

What exactly happened to Enoch?

What was it like the day the sun didn't go down?

When did Solomon start to go sour? Did he end up good or bad?

What was Satan really thinking when he started the war in heaven?

How many true followers were there in Jeremiah's day?

What was blasphemy of the Holy Spirit?

What did Paul mean by "baptism for the dead?"

What is the third heaven?

What about most of the book of Revelation?

Then it will be time to grab some time with the Hebrews-11 type heroes. First, I will thank them for inspiring me with their life, then on with the questions:

"Abel, did you know Cain was *that* angry?"

"Noah, how much help did you have with boat building? How did you get the rhinoceros on board?"

"Abraham, what did you do first when you found out Sarah was pregnant?"

"Joseph, what was it like in jail? Did you ever have a chance to escape?"

"Moses, did you ever think Pharaoh might outlast you?"

"Joshua, did you and Caleb struggle with any attitudes toward the faithless 10 who kept the Promised Land on hold for 40?"

"David, did you cry when you wrote Psalm 51?"

"Elijah, how did you outrun that chariot? A good short-cut, or were you an early Olympian?"

"Daniel, did you sleep, too, or just the lions?"

"Shadrach, Meshach, and Abednego (they will have to come together), what did you guys think about when you warmed yourself by a fire after the fire failed to burn you?"

"Ezekiel, did you remarry?"

"Jonah, what did you hang on to in there? Did Greenpeace originate in Nineveh?"

"Mary, did Jesus play organized sports? Did he ever get a spanking?"

"Joseph, where did you go? Did you die? How?"

"John the Baptist, did you and Jesus get much hang-time? What did you pray right before the sword reached your neck?"

"Andrew, what was it like being Peter's brother?"

"Peter, did you ever try walking on water again when nobody was watching? Did your kids get teased because dad was the key-holder?"

"Lazarus, what were you doing in Paradise when Jesus called you back to earth? How did you die—both times?"

"James and John, what did you and your mom discuss right after the right and left request was refused?"

"Stephen, did you think Saul would become Paul before you were killed?"

"Cornelius, did you and Peter stay close after your conversion? Did you ever eat pork together?"

"Barnabas, what did you do to become the Son of Encouragement?"

"Timothy, did your stomachaches eventually go away?"

"Luke, was it tough balancing your schedule between doctor and New Testament author?"

And then some time with those who lived from the first century through the 20th. To say thanks to the moms and dads who had the guts to say "Jesus is Lord" and then watch their sons and daughters become dinner for the starving dogs.

To hug the young man who refused to give in to parental pressure to quit the faith and was disowned and disinherited.

To listen to stories of those men and women who risked their lives and sneaked to their baptisms.

A few minutes would be nice with the catacomb churchgoers. Where was childcare? I bet the singing was great.

And then fellowship with any who daringly hid, smuggled

or died for the written word that now sits on my shelf available to me in the comfort of my home.

How did the disciples do during the Holy Wars?

Or the slaves who were abused and refused right to their rights? What was their secret to perseverance?

All of us together. From the first soul saved to the last soul saved, remembering, recounting, but most of all rejoicing that we made it.

But more than anyone else, I can't wait to see Jesus. Just Jesus. Oh, I know the line will be long. The hug line. The line we will all wait in to meet the Messiah.

The one we crucified. The one we ignored for so many years. What will I say when it's my turn? Will I have cottonmouth? Will I be speechless? What will he say to me? What will he look like? How long will we talk? There is so much I will want to tell him and thank him for. He's the reason I will have made it. I messed up so much, but he always stood up for me.

The long line won't matter either. No pushing. No shoving. No crowding. No bad backs. No sore feet. No sell-outs. Everyone will get in. No sighs of frustration because those in front are exceeding their time with the Lord. Just meet someone new in front of you and in back. Develop a new lifetime (eternal) relationship.

I hope to stand in line with my wife, the one who presently helps me most to make it. To joke about how close we came to divorce, but how God saw us through the trials. To laugh at times of delivery-room shouting, raising our kids, and our wedding day (not in that order). To see my second child who was taken at birth. Will Melissa be big? What will she look like? Are there children in heaven? How does that work? What about all the aborted babies? Surely God will bring up what others broke off. Will old people become young? Will we all be the same age? Twenty-two or twenty-three? Will we fly? Will we get to play sports (please!)? Does dreaming end? I know dates do. At least "I'm-looking-for-a-spouse" dates. How long is eternity? And where will God be? Probably the same place he has always been—everywhere.

My new body (prepare for major understatement) will be much better than it is now. Arnold, beware. For me, I hope to have thicker hair than Absalom. We baldies may be the happiest ones in heaven. Too bad we're not married. I'm quite sure our wives would have loved to run their fingers through our locks. My chest will be crowned with muscles. My biceps will bulge. I can flaunt without flexing. Handle-bars will become bars of granite. I am thrilled that a bicycle part will no longer describe the sides of my stomach. Spare tires will be changed and sit-ups will no longer be necessary. My stomach will stay firm without massive air intake. (Oh, come on—you do it, too!) "Chicken Legs" will cease to be my nickname. Right now, if you combined my left and right calves you would almost have one ordinary male calf. Or a female one, for that matter. My legs will be lean, loose and large. I will dunk and not be dreaming. My clothes will all fit. Perfectly. Belts will always stay buckled at the same hole. My breath will remain fresh, even in the morning. No more miniature dragons that find their way into my mouth. No glasses, no scars, no pains. Perfect.

I am also excited about what won't be there. Here is *my* list of heaven no-shows.

Flats. Car payments. Cars. Bill collectors. Bills. Jails. Prisons. Police blotters. Obituaries. Athlete's foot. Classi-fied ads. Hunger. Fruit cake. Construction. Schedules. Repentance. Potholes. Orange barrels. Traffic jams.

Pharmacies. Term papers. Speeding tickets. Speed traps. Car sales. Diets. Workout videos. Liver. Small, loud, bark-ing dogs. Horns. Sirens. Diapers. Dirty Diapers. Dirty, stinky diapers. Garbage dumps. Trash day. Trash. Weeds.

Junk mail. Bounced checks. Floating checks. Bank state-ments. Hospitals. Nursing homes. Age. Alarm clocks. Early mornings. Morning breath. Morning hair. Morning every-thing. Runny noses. Sinus problems. Homelessness. Pov-erty. Slums. Welfare. Food stamps.

Tee times. Slices. Hooks. Critical condition. Serious condition. Fair condition. Stubbed toes. Hangnails. Ingrown toenails. Deadlines. Riots. Politics. Campaigns. Advertisements. Talk shows. Ironing boards. Starch. Answering machines. Wrong numbers. Obscene phone calls. Phones. Rug burns. Floor burns. Burns. Board meetings. PTA meetings. Meetings.

Hypocrites. Religious confusion. Confusion. Pulpits. Hard rock with lousy lyrics. Water purifiers. Pimples. Gnats. Mosquitoes. Bites. Global warming. Ozone concerns. Pollution. Sympathy cards. Funeral music. Needles.

Frowns. Brady Bunch reruns. Possums. Skunk smell. Roadkill. Rumors of wars. Wars. Peace summits. Apologies. Sweat. Deodorant. Razors. Blisters. Envelope licking. Stamp licking. Unemployment lines. Unemployment. Employment. Resumes. Interviews. Insurance settlements. Insurance payments. Insurance.

Check-out times. Tow trucks. Death certificates. Forced laughter. Counselling. Bats. Snakes. Rats. Speed bumps. IRS forms, long or short. Gutter balls. Bowling alley odor. School lunches. Dorm food. Homework. Graduation speeches. Finals. Midterms. Studying. Security guards. Guns. Racial tension. Race. Jury duty. Guilty verdicts. Nightmares. Sleepless nights. Bad memories.

Toothaches. Dentistry. White-out. Menus. Curfews. Morning sickness. Delivery room pain. Delivery room panic. Batteries-not-included toys. Last-minute Christmas shopping. Language barriers. Cancelled flights. Airport confusion. All-points bulletins. Milk-carton children. Wheelchairs. Burned tongues. Marriage bumps. Divorce. Visitation rights. Custody battles.

Helmets. Glasses. Crutches. Hearing aids. Sign language. Vaccines. Drivers licenses. Drivers license photos. Social Security numbers. Fire alarms. False alarms. Cough syrup. Seeing-eye dogs. Gangs.

Cat scratches. Sunburn. Hot, warm, then cold showers. Laundromats. Bad jokes. Miscommunication. Bad news. Abortion. Drug deals. Credit applications. Flies at dinner time. Flies. Ants at picnics. Ants. Cockroaches. Interest.

Call-waiting. Too-cold air conditioning. Too-warm air conditioning. Air conditioning.

Temptation. Mid-life crisis. Locks. Keys. Accident reports. Accidents. Stitches. Diarrhea. White or pink diarrhea medicine. Bathroom scales. Bad report cards. Report cards. Dirty dishes. Fishing without catching. Neckties. Style. Fashion. Temper tantrums. Surgery. Waiting rooms. Strikes. Fasting. Poison labels. Protests. Used ashtrays. Ashtrays. Incest. Rape. Murder. Cancer. AIDS. Death.

What do you think? Go ahead. Write a hundred or two down.

Some may accuse me of having a wild imagination. Guilty as charged! But if the Scriptures are true that God really does give us more than we ask or imagine (Ephesians 3:20), I am in for an awesome eternity. I hope you will start imagining, too. Maybe heaven will be whatever we ask God for it to be. If so, you better start asking now. If it's not, and God gives us something completely different, I'm sure his plan will be much better than ours. But until I'm told exactly what heaven will be, my plans are to continue asking and dreaming. It has proven to be a blast!

Oh, we didn't discuss hell, did we? I'm not trying to avoid the subject, it is just as real to me as heaven. But words and phrases like "outer darkness," "weeping and gnashing of teeth," "separation" and "eternal fire" don't get me all that excited.

Hell. Satan's sanctuary of eternal fire fueled by pages of pornography and unused Bibles; bed sheets of adultery and immorality and the blankets that covered it; manuscripts of reporters' lies about God's people; articles of character assassination upon his radical leaders; cigarette cartons by the billions; playing cards that led gamblers to perish; and other highly flammable materials.

One atheist once said, "If hell were as real and as awful as Christians say it is, I would walk on my hands and knees on broken glass around the world just to tell one person to do everything he possibly could to avoid going there."

God is looking for the glass-walkers. It took a bloody Messiah to get us to heaven. The least we can do is give our hands and knees to save others from hell.

Heaven and hell. One holds promise. The other pain. One is a joy. The other a jail. Residents of one show their teeth. Residents of the other gnash theirs. Both have no opportunity to leave. Both are final. One is God's purpose for man. The other is Satan's. Choose God's purpose. Choose the purpose for which you were born. Choose heaven!

Chapter Five

The Journey

*"The God who made the world and everything
in it is the Lord of heaven and earth and does not live in
temples built by hands. And he is not served by human
hands, as if he needed anything, because he himself gives
all men life and breath and everything else. From one
man he made every nation of men, that they should
inhabit the whole earth; and he determined the times set
for them and the exact places where they should live"*
(*Acts 17:24-26*).

Life. A journey from the womb to the tomb. Ups
and downs, tosses and turns, growth and change,
eating, sleeping and just being you. A trip through
time. The time God has given you to be. A journey full of
sadness and surprises, people and problems, dreams and disappointments. A journey like none other. One we have no
opportunity to repeat. No trial examination. Only one shot.
Better make it good.

Talk about pressure. So much is at stake. Miss a basket,
no big deal. Miss life, you lose. Miss a putt, tap it in. Miss
life, pack it in. Too much pressure for most to handle. Read
the papers and you will see it is true. Breakdowns, blowups,
and bad decisions by the billions.

"Would someone please help me to figure out this thing
called life?"

Sound familiar? Life is a challenge but not an impossible one. Especially if you haven't already cut this chapter's opening passage out of your Bible.

"What is that?"

"Could that be true?"

"God is so involved in my life that he decided when I should be born and where I should live?"

We have only touched the hem. The garment remains.

Get ready for the ride of your life. Not the ferris wheel full of highs and lows that rivals the endurance of the Energizer bunny. Not the merry-go-round that keeps you busy but going nowhere. Pleasant sounds and pretty sights, but you'd like to graduate to something a little more exciting. Nor the scrambler that tosses you back and forth till you've bruised yourself permanently. No, this ride will thrill you, chill you, fill you—but never kill you. It is free. It is available. It is safe. But guaranteed: If you get on, you will not get off the same.

Only the bravest ride. The true thrill-seekers. Better get your seat belts on. Shoulder harness? Check. Now promise you won't ask to get off in the middle and you will keep your eyes open all the way. It makes it much more interesting.

"But I'm by myself. And it's a two-seater."

Don't worry, it is already occupied. God will be there. He has been on the ride many times before. He will even be happy to hold your hand if you need him to.

Okay, here we go. The slow, careful climb to the top of the hill. Just getting you ready for the ride of your life. Welcome to the roller-coaster of righteousness that won't make you sick. How's this for openers:

"For you created my inmost being; you knit me together in my mother's womb. I praise you because I am fearfully and wonderfully made; your works are wonderful, I know that full well. My frame was not hidden from you when I was made in the secret place. When I was woven together in the depths of the earth, your eyes saw my unformed body. All the days ordained for me were written in your book before one of them came to be" (Psalm 139:13-16).

"God, you were there too?"

You don't remember much of your womb wanderings, so God made sure you knew he was there. See your arms? God. See your legs? God. Eyes? God. Ears? God. Missing something? God. Whether it's all there, mostly there or hardly there, God was there. He had his reasons. If God were flesh, he would show up on every ultrasound.

And then it finally happens. Birth. Unfamiliar surroundings. You would like to go back in, but you exerted all your energy trying to stay in, and that didn't work. So you might as well stay. And there they are. Mom and Dad. Oh, it will be a number of months before you verbalize that, but you know a little about them. You have heard their voices. And besides, nobody else but Grandma wants to take you home, so you've decided to go along with it for now.

God came home, too. He knew who your parents would be. They were the ones he chose for you. Look beyond the purple polyester pants Dad embarrassed you with when he wore them to your school's open house, and beyond Mom's calling you "princess" 25 times when all your freshmen friends partied at your house, and Mom and Dad are probably okay. They bathed you, burped you, changed you and cuddled you. And in some way, roundabout or obvious, God used your parents—their strengths, their weaknesses, their jobs, their joys, their milestones and, yes, even their sin to get you to the point where you would give your life to your ultimate parent—God.

Granted, there were those times in my youth when I considered putting Mom and Dad up for adoption, but God knew I needed them. I learned servanthood watching my parents take care of their parents, while saying No to nursing home options. Dad would rise two or three times a night to help his father deal with numerous—and not so pleasant—medical problems. Mom waited hand and foot on her mother for about 10 years after her father's death. Rarely did I hear complaints.

Dad coached basketball for 20 years and for most of them was extremely successful. Two state championship teams, one third-place finish and now a member of the Washington State Coaches Hall of Fame. But he also had a few years where victories were as hard to come by as successful blind dates. Dad was always the same. I never remember seeing him down or blameshifting. Wins or losses, he remained steady. I am very thankful that God gave me my dad. I needed his example to be a strong leader in the church today. To understand that results, whether good or bad, do not *change who I am*. God was setting me up for success, and I did not even know it.

Well, maybe your mom and dad didn't care. Maybe you didn't have both. Maybe they yelled too much. They split up, and so you split time. They always fought in front of you. You logged more hours with the baby-sitter than you did with them. Dad was more interested in football on the couch than wrestling on the floor. Mom didn't take time to play school or attend the school play. Whatever the case, the truth still remains. *God* determined the time and the place for you to be born and the people and environment you were born to. Take a close look—you will see it too. God was there. He saw it all. And now he wants *you* to see it.

We are almost at the top. The first drop is right ahead. The drop that produces the phrase "I think I'm going to die." The times in your life when you thought you just could not go on. So bad you didn't *want* to go on.

Times of absolute embarrassment.

Long periods of loneliness.

Regrets.

Letting the team down.

Your best friend, or so you thought, told the very thing about you she had sworn to secrecy.

You got cut from the team?

You flunked your drivers test the first time?

Maybe you were forced to wear to school the "I would rather die than wear these" knickers Aunt Bertha gave you for your birthday.

A barbershop blunder that left you prematurely bald two days before school pictures.

We all have experienced the drops.

My first thoughts of death came during second grade show and tell. The evening before that dreaded morning, a second grade buddy named Robin came for what I thought would be a "typical" visit. My brother, 12 at the time and majoring in little-brother-bashing, gave Robin the inside scoop on what was inside my shirt. I was born with a birth defect, the medical term for which is *pectus excavatum*. A very small percentage of people have it. Mine just happened to be a severe case which left a massive cavity in my chest area.

"Show Robin the hole in your chest," he said.

I resisted at first, but thinking the excitement would die out quickly and life as usual would resume, I submitted. Robin was amazed, but as most seven year olds do, dropped it and looked for the next fun thing to do.

The following morning began as usual. Flintstones before school, cereal, catch the bus, playground pandemonium before the bell and then show and tell to start the day. I had my turn; Robin took his. I mentioned the hills we climbed; he mentioned the hole he found.

"I THOUGHT I WAS GOING TO DIE!!

But that, I would realize, was only the beginning. I was asked to go up on stage and show the class my hole. Sensitivity training was obviously missing from Mrs. James' education. Fellow second graders laughed. I felt as though, even after I pulled my shirt down, fifty eyes could see right through it. The school nurse came. The principal got involved. I'm surprised they didn't call an ambulance. I remember it vividly. How could you forget something like that? It changed my life. Me and my big hole, and Robin and his big mouth. Even Batman episodes were watched differently from that day forward as the Boy Wonder brought up memories of the show-and-tell fiasco.

God was a second grade teacher that day. He was there teaching me to be sensitive. He could have kept Robin from speaking. He didn't. He could have directed the teacher to show compassion. He didn't. Did he cause that moment? Did he allow it? It doesn't matter as long as I know he was there. That is all I need. I found some true friends that day and also learned that hearts can be badly broken by others' lack of tact and sensitivity.

My nickname, henceforth, was "Holy." I hated it at the time. If I had only known the implications. I am surprised I can still cry. I thought I lost a life's worth of tears that day. But I am still here, hole and all. I did not die after all.

And then there was the time the ball bounced off my head during a district basketball championship game my senior year of high school. (That's not normal in basketball but okay in soccer. I never played soccer.) We were up by one point with 15 seconds remaining. We had the ball and needed only to run out the clock. I was the ball handler, so the play designed was for me to inbound to Tim, then Tim to pass right back to me, I dribble around, three, two, one, zero, we win. Well, I got all the way to the part about inbounding the ball to Tim and then went brain dead. I forgot to look for the pass. Tim remembered to pass. Maybe God let the ball hit me in the head to get my brain working again. I hate telling the rest of the story, but I guess you must be dying to know. The other team got the ball, called time out, and scored with two seconds to go.

"I THOUGHT I WAS GOING TO DIE!!"

The locker room was simply a sweaty morgue. No sounds, just tears. Was it my mistake that cost us the game? You could not convince me otherwise then. You could now. God was there in the locker room. He was teaching me tons. He was teaching me about defeat. Not accepting it, but hating it. He was teaching me about memory and poise in key situations. He was teaching me that you can lose a good thing. Did God *cause* it? Did he *allow* it? It does not matter as long as I know he was there.

What was it for you?

Forget your lines in the school play?

Sing off-key during your first solo?

Freeze during the spelling bee championship?
Fumble on the potential game-winning drive?
Get held back in school?
Your first real girlfriend dumped you for no real reason?
Second girlfriend?
Third?
Find out you were adopted?
Dad or Mom was in the hospital and you saw his or her frailties for the first time?

It was scary, wasn't it? But you are still alive. God made sure. You survived the drop. Whether today you laugh, cry or become indifferent to the drops of life, God uses them to shape your life and ultimately get you to find him.

Now that the first drop is over, you can start climbing again. A breather. Gather yourself. The mini-vacations God gave you to keep you from the state of "overwhelment."

The summer at your grandparents' place, away from the hustle and bustle of home life. Summer camp. Slumber parties. Disney movies. Horseback riding. Good grades. Best friends in the back yard. Birthday parties. Pizza. Spring break. Snow days. Campfires. Marshmallow roasting.

Essential times of life that help bring the heart rate down and out of the dangerous beats-per-minute range. God knew you needed them. He knew how many you needed.

I moved to a new town only six months after the "Holy" chest controversy. Thank you, God. I scored the winning run in the state baseball championship game just three months after the ball-off-the-head-trick. Thank you, God. And so many more. Some I am aware of, most I am probably not.

The straight stretch. Fast and exciting, but nothing out of the norm. Just basic life. School, job, family, friends. Much of life is a straight stretch—we just don't realize it. Too often we are reliving and over-analyzing the drops so that the curves are upon us before we realize how long the straight stretch really was.

But here come the curves. You remember—when you are looking over the edge, and all you can do is hold on and pray, "Please don't let this car go off this track. I just want to live." It's fast. It hurts. It sometimes crushes.

Mom died, and she was your best friend.

Dad died, and you never really shared how much you loved him.

The divorce went through, and 30 days with Dad became three.

Your folks called the family together and announced another move—your third in five years. And you and Johnny had just made the sacred vow to be best friends.

Dad came into your room and touched you where you knew he shouldn't, but you didn't dare tell. After all, he was Dad.

Flunking classes. Few friends. Got beat up again. Bad biopsy results. Burns. Scars. Disease.

Mr. or Miss right said it was all wrong.

Your $30,000-a-year job was terminated.

Paralysis.

Lost a limb.

The loan fell through.

Your best friend died.

Your child got thrown in jail.

Miscarriage. Another miscarriage.

Negative pregnancy test. Another. Permanent.

Adoption became your option but you could not get the money. You got the money but could not find the child. You found the child, but the mother had second thoughts when she held the baby for the first time.

Dreams that died and now you would rather die than dream again.

God was there. He knew the hurt. Did he cause it? Did he allow it? I'm not sure. I am sure that all of it was meant to be used to get you home to heaven.

I am also convinced the Whys are not all that important. If God told us the whole truth, maybe we would believe half. Or, we may believe it but remain unsatisfied and critical. But if you choose to respond righteously to any challenge or difficult situation, and refuse to analyze and criticize God for his choices and allowances, life can actually be a joy to live.

My first curve came when I was 10. A family night with popcorn, pillows and blankets in front of the television. Mom, Dad, me and my sister Susie. My brother Tom would be joining us soon. He was with a friend but planned to be home later. Then the knock. The knock that knocked all of us down. My dad answered.

"Your son has been in an accident. He is hurt badly."

My parents rushed to the hospital. I cried. And cried some more. What happened? Would he be all right? Would he die? Only later would I realize how serious it was. My brother had been in a motorcycle accident. He was riding on the back without his helmet. For some reason, he had given his helmet to the driver. The driver broke his arm while Tom lay in a Portland, Oregon, hospital in critical condition. That was my brother. He lay in a coma for more than a month while my parents kept vigilant watch, overjoyed with the slightest twitch. I went to school, as usual, and classmates talked of death and brain damage. It was a long, hard curve.

Tom died. He was 15. I was 10. We fished together. I stopped. He took me hunting. I haven't gone since. I needed him. I loved him. He was my big brother. I missed him daily. I still miss him. It is hard to see a motorcycle without seeing Tom. Today's helmetless drivers call to mind the curve thrown my way almost 25 years ago. But God was there. Teaching me the importance of family. Introducing me to hospital pain. Giving me early lessons in Mom and Dad encouragement. Though not obvious at the time, I started to need God a lot more then. Maybe Jesus being a big brother (Hebrews 2:10-11) would be more appealing to me when my time came to decide.

Tom's funeral hurt. It was my first. At least the first I remember. I have attended many since. Both sets of grandparents have passed on. My sister-in-law's death was another curve. She was killed in an automobile accident when she was 28 and five months pregnant, leaving her husband and two small children behind. My baby's funeral was another curve. We had dreamed of a little girl and had gotten one. But she was dead on arrival. Did God cause all these events? Did God allow them? I may never know. I don't need to. Oh, granted, at times I look to find reasons. Sometimes I think of God's goodness. Other times I wrestle with the Why me?'s and get pinned consistently. But I know God was there, and that's good enough for me. And I know that God has used all these curves to keep *me* on the straight and narrow.

More straight stretch. You usually need it to put all your bones back in their proper place.

The job you always wanted. The spouse of your dreams. The raise. Two weeks in Hawaii. A best friend. A favorite hobby. Children. The dean's list. Your first house. A good book. Time that heals the hurts.

My dad became my best friend after Tom died. He still is. I often wonder what type of relationship we would have had if Tom were still here. I would do anything to change things and still have a big brother, but I would not change my friendship with my father for anything. Then God brought my wife and me closer than ever after her sister's death. I learned to care more, feel more and talk more—the three strikes for most husband hitters. Thank you, God. And he has been there in your life too.

Can you rattle off the straight stretches? Maybe you're on one right now. Maybe you're in a curve. Wherever you are, God is there. He's watching. He's scheming. He's protecting. He's disciplining. He's training. He's loving. He's listening. He's leading. All that has happened or will happen, God is well informed. He could have changed it all. He didn't. It's history. It's in the book. And it's all for one big reason. God is doing whatever he can to get *you* to heaven. In case you forgot, go back and read Chapter Four again. That's why you were born in that decade. That's why Mom and Dad are Mom and Dad. That's why God has allowed trials. That's why you are acquainted with death and suffering. God is getting you home.

We're not done yet. One more hill. The last drop. And it usually is the worst. None of us is there yet. It's whatever is in your future. The plans of God yet to be unfolded. The trials and tests that will strengthen you or stifle you. The persecution that pushes you on or persuades you to quit. It will come. It must. You will probably need to hold on tighter. Squeeze God's hand till it tells him you have learned to rely on him. Scream if you need to. But do not get off. You are almost done.

Will you be ready to pass the tests?

When your child at play forgets just once to look both ways. No more baths or bedtime stories. No trikes. No prom nights. No walking down the aisle.

When the telethon you used to watch for entertainment becomes the telethon at the top of your prayer list, and your son's muscles won't be needed on the gridiron anymore.

The sin you said you would never do, you did. Will you repent or run away?

The adultery opportunity that will be difficult to decline.

When handicapped parking spaces will become legal.

When your spouse says he or she will leave you if you don't leave the Lord.

Life can and will be painful. Two months can seem like two decades. Tears can flow hourly. But God has an ultimate destination in mind for us all. Seventy years will seem like seven seconds when your journey is over. And as you reach the gates of heaven and the door swings open so you can take that long-awaited first step into eternity, nothing will matter except that you believed God was there every step of the way and you refused to jump ship.

Only the last straight stretch remains. You are coming to the end of your ride. You made it! And because you realized God was in the seat next to yours, you prayed, but did not panic; you trusted, but did not tense up; and you gulped, but did not get off.

When your ride ends, you close your eyes, rest your body, and retire from your journey. God will pick you up and carry you to where you always wanted to be in the first place. Heaven. The journey is over.

I don't know about you, but this ride thrills me. To think that God knows and cares for my every move and works for my benefit—what attention! To think that God orders the events of my life, asks angels to assist me, changes bad to good, and holds Satan at arm's length sends chills up my spine like listening to the "Star Spangled Banner" before the big game. An all-powerful God with wrath and mercy at his fingertips has chosen to give me his hand, work for my good and give me the chance of a lifetime. But first, I must take the ride of a lifetime.

It starts in the womb and ends in the tomb. In between, you get God.

Chapter Six

The Bible

*"And we have the word of the prophets made more
certain, and you will do well to pay attention to it, as to a
light shining in a dark place, until the day dawns and the
morning star rises in your hearts. Above all, you must
understand that no prophesy of scripture came about by
the prophet's own interpretation. For prophesy never
had its origin in the will of man, but men spoke from God
as they were carried along by the Holy Spirit"*

(2 Peter 1:19-21).

Rumors.
Mere possibilities presented as absolutes. Information most often believed as factual with little investigative efforts. Hearsay evidence. So-called truths derived from acute emotion rather than accurate information. We are being served platefuls every day. And too many of us sit down to eat.

"Well so-and-so told me so, so it must be so."

"You are kidding?"

"NO!!"

"REALLY?"

"WOW!!"

God knew there would be rumors. Information passed along through the ages about the Creator. Some true. Some false. Some vague. Some clear. Some good. Some bad. The problem—SOME.

Thank God the printing presses were warming before Adam arrived. A book about God was being bound and bound to reach every human's eye. Filled with pages of descriptive material about its author. No rumors—just truth. No possibilities—just facts.

The Bible. The rumor-buster and fact-finder. I have learned to hate rumors over the years. Especially the ones about me. They hurt. They damage my reputation. Come meet me. Walk with me. Talk to me. Investigate me. But please do not spread rumors about me.

God must have incredible patience. So many lies and half-truths have been spoken about him throughout the ages. Lies and rumors that ruin his reputation and, in turn, ruin many lives. Meet God. Walk with God. Talk to him. Investigate him. *Read your Bible.*

The only book ever written that stands alone. If all you had was a Bible, you would be set for life. It will introduce you to God—his nature, his plans and his expectations. The #1 Best-Seller. The book that everybody buys but few finish. More than likely, it's in your home. On a bookshelf. On a coffee-table. In your bedroom. In a box. A bathroom magazine rack. A closet. An attic. A cellar. Aladdin's Lamp wanting to be found and rubbed. A hidden treasure with unlimited potential. A life-changer.

Many days have come and gone when you moved in its direction, but rumors reared their ugly heads, so you opted for the romance novel or the athlete's autobiography.

"It's too difficult to really understand anyway."

"As long as you believe it's true that's enough."

"You don't really need to study it."

If these Satanic suggestions haven't stopped you, maybe the excuses have:

"I don't really have the time right now."

"I tried once but didn't get much out of it."

Or the lies of Lucifer that reach your lips:

"I will start tomorrow."

"I'll get around to it one of these days."

"When things finally settle down at work, then I'll start."

"I've read it before, so I already know what it says."

But many of us denounced the demon of rumors. We found our Bible. We picked it up. We closed our eyes; fanned the pages till we felt something compel us to stop; straightened our index finger; waved it; lowered it; and then placed it.

"This is it! I know this will change my life."

But we discovered the blood of bulls and goats on temple curtains sprinkled by high priests in the order of Melchizedek found little practical application for our 20th-century chaos. So the finger-finders, once rumor-refusers, are now tempted to spread rumors.

Or the "I base my life and belief in God on one Scripture" people. John 3:16 idolatry. Worshipping the scripture but not the "Scriptor."

Behind-the- goal-post gurus convinced that their sign will convince you to sign up with God.

Or the people who fashion their God first, then find the first scripture that agrees. Looking for agreement without agreeing to look.

Just a few examples of the modern methods of God-making that happen with regularity. Risky at best. Eternal damnation at worst.

God gave us the Bible to read. He put boatloads of information about himself throughout its pages. It is so simple we miss it. God wrote a book so we would know exactly who he is. A book inundated with truth about his exact nature.

Let's meet up close and personal the God of the universe. The God of the Bible. This God stands tall, proud and available. If you have created any other gods, decide now to sit them down and keep them there.

For approximately six months before starting this book, I read through the entire Bible, looking simply for verses that described God. Verses inspired by God so there would be no confusing the matter. I underlined each one (I'm sure I missed a bunch!), then went back to examine and analyze what I had underlined. Now, granted, you can't put God in a box, package him and send him off. But certainly you can understand him. Certainly he wants us to. I believe God is understandable and explainable to a large degree. Contained in this and the next three chapters are my observations on the nature of God. I will explain the six main qualities of God found in abundance in the pages of the Bible and why I believe God wants us to see these qualities. In Chapters Seven, Eight, and Nine we will take a peek at my "Top 10" passages in these six areas, first from the Old Testament, then the New, and, finally, the Psalms.

Here goes. The God of the Bible. From God himself.

1) God is holy.

He is above everything. Nothing and nobody compares to him. He is "set apart" from all else because he is God. He is not human. He is not an angel. He is not bound by anything. Time and space mean absolutely nothing to him. Nobody orders him. He has no creator. He is God.

When will you need to be reminded of a holy God?

Every time you try to make him human while elevating yourself to deity.

Every time you think God is merely "run-of-the-mill" and praying to him and reading about him is undesirable and uneventful.

When you are bored with life and think God is sleeping too.

When you think time is running out and God operates by stopwatch.

2) God is powerful.

He can do anything he wants at any time he wants anyway he wants. What challenges man's intellect insults God's intelligence. His invisible fingertips contain more power than 10 billion visible hands. Saturday morning superhero stunts are a mere drop in a world-sized bucket to what God can do. Unlimited. Impressive. The 'S' spans his universal chest. He is powerful. He is God.

You will need routine reminders of a powerful God that can light the soul during spiritual blackout and water the heart during spiritual famine.

"I've always been this way. I don't believe I can change." Plug in.

"Do my prayers really matter?" Plug in.

The times in ICU when countless tubes tell a chilling tale. Plug in.

When the divorce papers have fresh ink, but you lack a fresh perspective. Plug in.

When you doubt you can do what God tells you to do. Plug in.

When you need to admit the truth about what really happened but are so terrified of the recovery period. Plug in.

3) God is good.

As God, he can be whatever he wants to be. I am glad he chose to be good. Every move ever made by God, every decision ever derived by God, every act ever enacted by God is good. No bad, or hint thereof, can be found in God. His thoughts. His intentions. His discipline. His choices. All are ultimately good. He even turns the evil of Satan into good. He is good. He is God.

Understanding the goodness of God is also key to joyful living. God knows you will need a healthy dose of "good God" Scriptures.

When death knocks at doors of friends' and families' houses.

When you lose your job a day after you closed on the house.

When you are doing the same things this month as last, but results are nowhere to be found.

When persecution comes your way after doing what's right and tempts you to wonder if you're all wrong.

4) God is caring.

He proves his good nature by his actions. He hurts for

us. He knows our difficulties. His flexibility is uncanny as he regularly bends over backwards to help us and stoops down to relate. He walks with the weak, hugs the heavy-hearted, hangs out with the orphans, and delivers the downcast. He walks ahead of mankind to clear trouble and temptation out of the way. He walks behind man to pick him up when he falls and encourage him to go on, carrying him if need be. And he walks on each side, holding each hand to assure man that all will be okay. Every situation. Every hurt. Every need. Every tear. Every funeral. Every hospital. He is caring. He is God.

And how many times will we need to be assured that God cares? That we are not alone and he is on our side? Maybe you have already been there.

The drunk driver who lived while your firstborn died. The judge suspended his license while you suspended all normal activity.

The high school prom that you weren't asked to, so instead, you, along with fellow failures, planned a loser's party and drowned your sorrows with the beer you forced yourself to drink.

The custody battle you lost for your daughter. You told the truth. Your former spouse lied. You lose.

The chemotherapy that cuts like a knife and sends you to the hat store looking for some dignity.

When live reports from famine-stricken Africa are brought to your living room and you wonder why God gave any of those children room to live. Skeleton kids by the millions looking for food and some flesh on their bones.

A holy God. A powerful God. A good God. A caring God. Few problems so far. Take a deep breath. We are coming to the wall. The monster all distance runners meet on their way to the finish line. The wall of decision. Do I go on, or do I stop? Let's go on.

5) God is hard-line.
He calls the shots. He has expectations. His first four

qualities require all to welcome his teachings and expectations without hesitation. His position cannot be taken. His plans cannot be voted on. A recall or impeachment is out of the question. He is not soft or cushy. He is not wimpy. He cannot be walked on. Compromise is not in his vocabulary. God is a God of *musts* not *maybes*, *have to*s not *try to*s. God is hard. There is a line. He is hard-line. He is God.

"Expectation" and "commitment" will never be popular words among the masses, but they scatter themselves throughout God's written word.

The coach's game plan. The teacher's syllabus. The *dos* and *don't*s of deity. Absolutes of the Almighty. Commandments, not suggestions. Ideals, not ideas.

For all the times we don't feel like doing it. The moments in our lives when we believe feelings supersede truth.

When we look for a church that suits our beliefs rather than looking for truth and then finding a church that follows it.

When you are more into admiring Jesus than imitating him.

When God becomes good friend, buddy and pal without being Maker, Lord and Master.

When you are tempted to soften the blow on a potential knockout-punch scripture while studying the Bible with a close friend.

When thoughts of "I'm OK, you're OK" seem OK.

You will need to go back to your Bible and get reacquainted with a hard-line God.

6) God is just.
To those who refuse to honor his holiness, God is just, and consequently will show his wrath. For any who doubt and diffuse his power, God shows his wrath. For the self-seekers who abuse his goodness, God shows his wrath. To all those who expect God to care without expecting themselves to care, God shows his wrath. For any who walk softly on God's hard line, God shows his wrath. Not his choice, but ours. Granted, this is the last quality God wants to exercise, but by refusing to carry out wrath, he ceases to be God.

Hardened hearts. Hopelessness. Hell. Samples of the wrath of God. Expressed every day in various degrees, God's wrath is obvious in our world and in your Bible. He is wrathful when he needs to be. He is God.

Wrath. Punishment. Destruction. Severe suffering. Hellfire. Brimstone. Lake of fire.

Designed for those who are one step away from falling away.

For any who have packed their spiritual suitcases with emptiness and are just about to leave for vacation away from the God of the Bible.

Or for those who utter foolish statements like "Hell won't be that bad. God's probably just using scare tactics to get us in line."

When purgatory becomes a hope.

When you believe the make-believe.

When you climb into bed with a unvowed-to woman and believe it's not that bad.

When you choose to sin in any capacity and fully expect that God will forgive you.

When possible punishment seems ludicrous. God has become Mr. Nice Guy while you are anything but.

When death could never happen to you.

To those who believe AIDS is an accident, homosexuality is an alternative lifestyle and sex before marriage is helpful in securing the right partner.

When phrases like "extra-martial affair," "gay rights" and "pro-choice" are positives in your dictionary of life.

There will be wrath. And we all need to hear it. What are your ears itching to hear?

God is so much else. He is emotional, but will never need the counseling couch. He rewards, but never spoils to our downfall. He has got grace galore and loves to give it out. He will test us, but never unfairly. And the "What is God like?" list goes on.

These are the facts. At least the ones I have found. Facts tell the truth. Rumors are only rumors. So don't let your

God be a rumor. Get a Dragnet Deity. "Just the facts, ma'am."
    Fall in love with the God of love. You will find him in the
Bible.

Chapter Seven

The Old

"For everything that was written in the past was written to teach us, so that through endurance and the encouragement of the Scriptures we might have hope"
(Romans 15:4).

The Old Testament.
Hundreds of chapters. Thousands of verses. More than 1,000 years from first writer to last.
Creation to captivity.
Raising Cain to falling walls.
Righteous Abel and the offering table.
Big boats and little faith.
Ouches of circumcision to *oohs* and *aahs* of the Promised Land.
A father teaching his son about sacrifice.
A mother floating her son to stardom.
A youngster with guts and rocks gaining a kingdom.
A maiden's beauty and bravery foiling plans for an early Holocaust.
The Ark. The Ark of the covenant.
A Pharaoh's repentance. A Pharaoh's immersion.
Garden of Eden. Gardens of Babylon.
Temples built. Temples destroyed. Temples built again.
Talking donkeys. Low-flying quail. Blood-hungry dogs.
Water. Lots of water.
Blood. Lots of blood.

Wars. Lots of wars.

Fire that does not burn.

Lions that do not bite.

Splitting seas. Floating axheads.

Armies routed with ancient noisemakers. Cities destroyed with stomps and shouts.

The Old Testament. Pages littered with excitement and drama. But in all your eagerness to know the events of the Old, do not miss the obvious—God. He is all over the place. He is introduced and explained. And he, more than all the events surrounding him, is exciting. Take a glance at the following Scriptures in David Letterman style. Here are my "Top 10" verses from the six qualities of God discussed in Chapter Six.

God Is Holy

10) *"To whom will you compare me? Or who is my equal?" says the Holy One"* (Isaiah 40:25).

Can you think of anyone? Ghandi? God *never* eats! Abraham Lincoln? God put him in office. Besides, the more you know about history's Hall of Famers, the more you discover their inadequacies. The more you know of God, the more you discover why this scripture is Top 10 material.

9) *"How great is God—beyond our understanding! The number of his years is past finding out"* (Job 36:26).

During my two years in Cincinnati, I looked forward to the few trips we took as a family to the Kings Island amusement/theme park. Of the hundreds of "win a $10 stuffed animal on only a $100 effort" rip-off booths, my wife and I always anticipated an automatic win at the "Guess Your Age" stand. The person in charge would do their best to discern your age within two years and if he failed, you win the prize of your choice. It sounds somewhat difficult, but amazingly, they were correct a high percentage of the time. But incorrect every time Patty appeared. She was 28 on her first attempt to fool. She looked then, and still does, to be about

18-22. Even though we weren't champions at tossing the ring around the bottle and still to this day have never knocked down all the necessary pins to win any prize, we always were confident in promising the kids at least one small token of our visit there, won from the hapless age-guesser.

What if God stepped up to the booth? What would be your best guess? One million years? Nice try, but give God a teddy bear. How about one billion years? Oh, rats, you just barely missed it by several billion. One trillion? Hand it over; the inflatable baseball bat now belongs to God. A zillion? A million zillion? You could try guessing God's age each second of each day for the rest of your life and still never come close to the correct answer: "past finding out."

8) *"God understands the way to it [wisdom] and he alone knows where it dwells, for he views the ends of the earth and sees everything under the heavens"* (Job 28:24).

We spend lifetimes and millions to get our few tidbits of wisdom. God gives it away. We pray for it and are willing to pay for it. God is it. The wise one who's more than willing to share his secrets.

7) *"God is not a man, that he should lie, nor a son of man, that he should change his mind. Does he speak and then not act? Does he promise and not fulfill?"* (Numbers 23:19).

Find just one human without a lie on his or her record. Find one who was always true to his or her promises. One who finished everything started. Staying in the upper percentile in any of these areas would be commendable. How do you do?

Sixty percent? Maybe.

Seventy percent? Check again.

Eighty? Doubt it.

Ninety? Liar.

One hundred percent? God.

6) *"How great you are, O Sovereign LORD! There is no one like you, and there is no God but you, as we have heard with our own* *ears"* (2 Samuel 7:22).

"Great" describes about anything these days. Great game! Great meal! Great news! Great deal! Great date! "Great" only because we have so much mediocre and ordinary to compare it to. What if God played quarterback? What if God cooked dinner? At best, a few things about us are good. At worst, all things about God are great.

5) *"But will God really dwell on earth? The heavens, even the highest heavens, cannot contain you"* (1 Kings 8:27).

Big and Tall shops have nothing near his size. Texas, move over. There is something bigger and better. Not bad for no flesh.

4) *"I will proclaim the name of the LORD. Oh, praise the greatness of our God! He is the Rock, his works are perfect and all his ways are just. A faithful God who does no wrong, upright and just is he"* (Deuteronomy 32:3-4).

God owns no erasers. He has no need for white-out. No spellcheck will be found on his computer. It is nice to know that in a world of mistakes, the world leader is exempt.

3) *"'Am I only a God nearby,' declares the LORD, 'and not a God far away? Can anyone hide in secret places so that I cannot see him?' declares the LORD. 'Do not I fill heaven and earth?' declares the LORD"* (Jeremiah 23:24).

X-ray vision minus the eyeballs! In a cave? God knows every bat. Under a bed? God was there before the boogey man. In a closet? God is hanging somewhere. Wherever you go, there is God.

2) *"'But how can a mortal be righteous before God? Though one wished to dispute with him, he could not answer him one time out of a thousand. His wisdom is profound, his power is vast. Who has resisted him and come out unscathed?'"* (Job 9:2-4).

The ultimate umpire. Angry with his call? You said Safe! and God said Out?

OUT!!

A call based on absolute wisdom. No instant replay necessary. Don't bother kicking the dirt. (You can't hit spirit!)

1) *"So listen to me, you men of understanding. Far be it from God to do evil, from the Almighty to do wrong. He repays a man for what he has done; he brings upon him what his conduct deserves. It is unthinkable that God would do wrong, that the Almighty would pervert justice. Who appointed him over the earth? Who put him in charge of the whole world?"* (Job 34:10-13).

Imagine trying to lead God. Most of us do not need to imagine. We have tried it many times. Stop trying. Your experience is severely limited. Hit your knees, and surrender your seat. Bow your head and feel your crown fall. There is room for one king. Just enough gems for one crown. One throne sat upon by the One who has been there for all eternity—God.

God Is Powerful

10) *"Yet their Redeemer is strong; the LORD Almighty is his name. He will vigorously defend their cause so that he may bring rest to their land, but unrest to those who live in Babylon"* (Jeremiah 50:34).

The ultimate in protection perfection. A 24-hour, no-sleep, never-eat bodyguard willing to take the bullets but not the bucks.

9) *"There is no wisdom, no insight, no plan that can succeed against the LORD"* (Proverbs 21:30).

Got any go-after-God plans? Think them out. Write them down. Refine them. Act upon them. Foiled. God knew your thoughts before you did. God had your plans on file before your birth certificate was on file. Your best bet—surrender.

8) *"And he became more and more powerful, because the LORD God Almighty was with him"* (2 Samuel 5:10).

For all those suffering from less-and-less syndrome:

"My marriage is less and less fulfilling."

"My life is less and less exciting."

"My children are less and less obedient."

"My joy is less and less obvious."

"My fun times are less and less frequent."

"My friendships are less and less helpful."

More and more medication is available. While you run on empty, God's medicine cabinet is always full. Go grab a bottle or two and start living.

7) *"In everything he did he had great success, because the LORD was with him"* (1 Samuel 18:14).

God has never participated in "most-everything" ministry. The ultimate meddler, he hopes to butt in on every area of our lives. To touch your job and not your joy is not of God. His invisible fingers are thick enough to touch both. To take your pain but not your pressure is not a part of his plan. God's holy hands are big enough to grab both.

6) *"He does what he pleases with the powers of heaven and the peoples of the earth. No one can hold back his hand or say to him 'What have you done?'"* (Daniel 4:35).

The sun-setter, moon-maker, Satan-slayer and people-planner. He brings rain by decision, not dance. If God wants snow, white flakes fall. Hurricanes and tornadoes are nothing but miniature puffs from the mouth of God. The devil deals a bad hand to mankind only after God allows approval. Trying to stop God is about as futile as a Lex Luther plan for world conquest during a Kryptonite famine.

5) *"Even if you go and fight courageously in battle, God will overthrow you before the enemy, for God has the power to help or to overthrow"* (2 Chronicles 25:8).

How many do you suppose are in God's army? Would you like to compare strategies with the Red Sea Remover? Got any bombs with the destructive capabilities of a dropped sun?

Now, granted, to possess courage is an added advantage in any of life's battles. But courage never appears in any win/loss column. You may have tremendous courage—perhaps enough to be presented a purple heart for one of those battles—but without muscle, intellect and weaponry, plan on losing most of the time. Don't drop the courage, just add some wisdom. Go grab God, and get back in the battle.

Need help with the kids? Don't be content with the parent purple heart. You fought, overcame wounds, and survived, but lost the kids. Go get them back—with God this time.

Need help dealing with the past? The past purple heart is available. For survivors of wounds from abuse, lack of parental love, alcoholism and other basic dysfunctional dilemmas. You've stayed alive long enough to talk about it in group. You even raise your family today with different standards. But your wounds seem to require regular bandages because you're still unwilling to surrender to God's painful, but successful, surgery called complete forgiveness.

Help is available. Recipes of revival are available for life's discouraged and down-and-out. Read them, do them and watch God win in your life.

4) *"Do you not know? Have you not heard? The LORD is the Everlasting God, the Creator of the ends of the earth. He will not grow tired or weary and his understanding no one can fathom. He gives strength to the weary and increases the power of the weak"* (Isaiah 40:29).

God pulls continual all-nighters without next-day nap requirements. Weak-willed? God's strong will warehouse managers are looking for "I won't give up" orders to fill. Weak bodied? Fresh flesh requests are rarely dishonored. Weak-kneed? Angels known throughout heaven for their boldness hover over earth's scaredy-cats while keeping the barking dogs tied to their trees.

3) *"With your help I can advance against a troop; with my God I can scale a wall"* (2 Samuel 22:30).

David scaled the giant wall with faith and five smooth stones. He scaled the repentance wall with confession of sin and an absence of complaining when punishment proceeded. He scaled the wall of persecution with humility, patience and constant cheek-turning.

Walls. We all have them. Walls that we've tried to climb numerous times, only to drop down each time to the bottom.

The walls erected that come between marriage and marital bliss. You have climbed with counselors full of ideas but silent on Scriptures. You have climbed with separate vacations hoping to come back different people—only to see you will need a permanent one. You have climbed with a mutual decision to be fruitful and multiply only to see the kids complicate the situation.

You erected walls that separated you from your potential. You surrounded yourself with leaders but not the Lord. You snorted the coke so many times you could no longer smell victory. You relived your past continually and convinced yourself you had no real future. You failed in key situations, and decided the wall-climbing rope would only burn you again.

So many walls. It's a world of walls. And God is a God of ropes. God provides them. You climb them. Non-breakable ropes entwined with Scripture, Spirit, salvation and security. Grab ahold, and start scaling.

2) *"On the day the LORD gave the Amorites over to Israel, Joshua said to the LORD in the presence of Israel, 'O sun, stand still over Gibeon, O moon, over the valley of Aijalon.' So the sun stood still and the moon stopped, till the nation avenged itself on its enemies,' as it is written in the Book of Jashar. The sun stopped in the middle of the sky and delayed going down about a full day. There has never been a day like it before or since, a day when the LORD listened to a man. Surely the LORD was fighting for Israel"* (Joshua 10:11-14).

Oh, to have been there on that day. Or was it two days? An early version of daylight-savings time. A day longed for by all beached sun worshippers. God's revolving earth rests momentarily in his heavenly holster. Extra time needed to win the battle.

Too busy? Limited on time? Losing some battles? God may not stop the earth again, but the possibility of a "never been a day like it" for your life still remains.

1) *"Be strong and courageous. Do not be afraid or discouraged because of the king of Assyria and the vast army with him, for there is a greater power with us than with him. With him is only the arm of flesh, but with us is the* LORD *our God to help us and to fight our battles.' And the people gained confidence from what Hezekiah the king of Judah said"* (2 Chronicles 32:7-11).

Confidence. We all need it; we all look for it. But we seldom find it. What we need is a boost. Better yet, a big brother. The cocky fifth-grade bullies have mocked our second-grade status. You've encountered the bullies, I'm sure.

The billboards, advertisements, magazine covers and high school heater-leaners shouting—"Unless you're gorgeous, you're a geek."

The bullies of child molestation keeping you from enjoying sex with your spouse.

The racist bullies that honor skin color more than qualification, keeping you at minimum wage and maximum rage.

Don't grab the makeup or the phone number of your local plastic surgeon. Don't yell inwardly at Mom and Dad and then outwardly at your marriage partner. Don't spend time blaming society or dreaming of a different world.   Instead, take your small second-grade hand and clasp the huge hand of an already graduated God. Then watch the fifth-grade bullies leave one at a time. And they will never be back.

God Is Caring

10) *"For many years you were patient with them. By your Spirit you admonished them through your prophets. Yet they paid no attention, so you handed them over to the neighboring peoples. But in*

*your great mercy you did not put an end to them or abandon them,
for you are a gracious and merciful God"* (Nehemiah 9:30-31).

Check this out. We blow it. We keep on blowing it. We
get help, and we still blow it. We get punished and blow it
some more. And all the while, God remains patient. He
sends help. He disciplines in hope that we will change. He is
patient again. He is patient once more. God has the uncanny ability to hang with people who are hanging themselves. Like the father who refuses to believe all the solid
evidence and confirmed reports condemning his son to a
life of losing. So, too, God is completely unwilling to call it
quits on anyone who has heartbeats remaining.

9) *"When the LORD saw that Leah was not loved, he opened
her womb, but Rachel was barren"* (Genesis 29:31).

God has a way of keeping us encouraged. The Bible describes Leah as having "weak [or delicate] eyes" (Genesis
29:17)—a polite way of saying she was somewhat unattractive. Rachel, on the other hand, had the looks and thus, the
lock on the boys. But Leah's lack of second-lookers brought
God onto the scene. So, instead of winks and whistles, she
got a working womb.

God is always at the doorstep of the unsanctioned, but
still-operating, orphanages.

The "nobody likes me—everybody hates me—I think I'll
go eat worms" adoption agencies.

The "I never got asked to the homecoming dance" orphanage.

The "I got cut from the team" orphanage.

The "Mom and Dad didn't have much time for me" orphanage.

The "I'm overweight and unattractive" orphanage.

The "I have no marketable skills" orphanage.

The "my spouse left me for another" orphanage.

Orphanages are everywhere. So is God. Not there just
to visit. He is ready to sign the papers and take you home.

Every time Leah felt the movement of life in her midsection, she was reminded that the same God who commands orphanage visitations (James 1:27) was there when she wept in hers.

What don't you have that others have that you wish you had? Whatever the answer, God cares enough to give you more in other areas to keep discouragement demons at a distance.

8) *"By day the LORD went ahead of them in a pillar of cloud to guide them on their way and by night in a pillar of fire to give them light, so that they could travel by day or night"* (Exodus 13:21).

Promised Land pursuers with chariot clouds and fiery flashlights.

Not much is worse than not knowing where to go. My son Bradley was playing in his first organized baseball game three summers ago and because of bad weather, his team had not had the opportunity to practice more than once or twice. Consequently, some of the basics of baseball, like baserunning, were missing. So six-year olds, when unsure of their next step, take it anyway, not knowing where they will end up.

In his first official at-bat, Bradley hit the ball to the short-stop. Now, if you have seen pee-wee baseball lately, you know that bunts can easily become home runs. Kids just keep running till they get tagged and usually that occurs on the bench when teammates slap them "five" for their first round-tripper.

Bradley took off for first. The throw. Overthrow of course.

"Go to second," I yelled.

But Bradley took to the route of right field. Nobody was in his way. No tags were possible. Why not? Had my wife not restrained me, I would have carried him to second myself to save the embarrassment. Not his. Mine. I think a young angel who had been there before picked him up and scooted him toward the appropriate base.

The throw. Overthrow number two.

"Go, Bradley!" I exclaimed.

I forgot to say "to third." So he took the shortest route between two points—a straight line from second to home. Why bother with third? The coach (who was also the pitcher) grabbed him and pointed him to third. He made it. He scored on the next play.

Life is a lot like running bases. Unless you know the rules, you can get lost. Or you can decide to make up your own rules along the way. Either way, you end up losing the game. Bradley learned quickly. He got taught. First the angel in right field, then the adult on the mound. Dad jumped in there, too, and now base-running blunders are at a minimum.

Who is teaching you? God has plenty of modern day clouds available. Simple direction in the daylight. Pillars of fire are also plentiful. Gentle nudges in the nighttime.

Whether in a car or a career, direction is a much-welcomed commodity. Never was there a day when God's people did not know where to go. Clouds were no longer discussions on the latest weather fronts but the newest frontiers for Israel. Fire was not a sign of tragedy but a signal to travel. Moveable pillars permanently sunk in the foundation of truth—God cares and looks to lead your life.

Twenty-four hours a day God longs to tell us exactly how to get to second base. Then third. Home is where he stands with a welcome sign.

7) *"Then I said to you, 'Do not be terrified; do not be afraid of them. The LORD your God, who is going before you, will fight for you, as he did for you in Egypt, before your very eyes, and in the desert. There you saw how the LORD your God carried you, as a father carries his son, all the way you went until you reached this place'"* (Deuteronomy 1:29-31).

God—the first "male carrier." Just ask Adam. And he has been carrying mankind ever since.

Tired? Sick? Sick and tired? Need a lift? On your back? Did you feel that?

"Who picked me up?"

That was God, of course.

"Where is he taking me?"

Where every good father takes his child when he's tired. To a place that is secure and comfortable. A bed of rest. A bed of recovery.

There is nothing like taking my daughter when she is sleeping (and about 10 pounds heavier), draping her over my shoulders and climbing the stairs to transfer her to her final resting place. I get a good workout and she gets a good night's sleep. Is it a burden? Only a bad back the following day comes close. God does it for all of us regularly with no next-day need for Doan's Pills.

6) *"It was I who taught Ephraim to walk, taking them by the arms; but they did not realize it was I who healed them. I led them with cords of human kindness, with ties of love; I lifted the yoke from their neck and bent down to feed them"* (Hosea 11:3-4).

God would unquestionably be the total parent. Holding our arms, he would teach us how to walk. He would be there for our first step, his continually-running camcorder in hand. There, as well, for our second and third steps. He would cheer as we proceeded all the way across the room, his holy arms extended in case of possible falls. Life's coffee tables would be moved aside, eliminating frustration and possible injury. Plenty of applause would be heard accompanied by a reassuring smile and rewards for jobs well done.

He would enroll us in the school of life, take us and pick us up on Day One, and make sure we were secure at all other times. He would check our report cards, watch our games, meet our teachers, plan parties for our classmates, monitor our progress, listen to our fears and hear our complaints. God would carry our photo in his universal wallet and boast of our accomplishments. He would make our lunches or supply the lunch money. God would offer help with the homework but make us learn, tolerating the 'C's when full effort was given. He would sympathize with the peer pressure and steer us from nerddom; laugh when we laughed; cry when we cried; and beam when we graduated.

God has been there from beginning to the present in your school of life. He parents like none other. Don't cut classes. Don't quit. Get some good teachers, and learn from your regular report cards. On judgment day, heaven will be your diploma.

5) *"You give me your shield of victory; you stoop down to make me great. You broaden the path beneath me, so that my ankles do not turn"* (2 Samuel 22:36-37).

The heavenly trainer keeping us from life's painful sprains. In sports it's exercise, stretching, tape jobs, hightop shoes and swept floors. With God it's a Bible to teach us. A conscience to warn us. A friend to help us up along the way. A victory to inspire us. A defeat to humble us. A death to touch us.

The wrap jobs of God. Divine protection on the tough and bumpy road called Life, lined with demons in the ditches ready and waiting to trip you up.

4) *"'For your Maker is your husband–the LORD Almighty is his name–the Holy One of Israel is your Redeemer; he is called the God of all the earth. The LORD will call you back as if you were a wife deserted and distressed in spirit–a wife who married young, only to be rejected,' says your God. 'For a brief moment I abandoned you, but with deep compassion I will bring you back'"* (Isaiah 54:5-7).

The Israelites had completely blown it. They married the one of their dreams, then forced God's signature on divorce papers as adultery annulled the vows. God had no choice, but as always, was using even this tragic occasion to bring about victory. He was not willing to remarry in hopes his second altar appearance would again be with his first wife. The God of the second chance. Need one?

Aborted a baby in your womb? God will be waiting in the delivery room next time.

Failed in marriage? God would love to give you away to one of his faithful followers this time.

Bring up your kids wrong? God has got glue galore and is ready to restore broken or shattered dreams.

Adultery? God shouts, "DAVID!"
Liar? "JACOB!"
Murder? "PAUL!"
Denial? "PETER!"
All brought back from the pit with a huge rescue chain called compassion.

3) *"He tends his flock like a shepherd: he gathers the lambs in his arms and carries them close to his heart; he gently leads those that have young"* (Isaiah 40:11).

(From someone who hates the 20th-century's blue-eyed, blond-haired Jesus carrying a lamb, I still felt I could not pass by this incredible scripture.)

He tends. Gathers. Carries. Leads. God, the Shepherd of shepherds. No kicking or prodding. Instead, you are gathered in his arms, carried comfortably and cozily by a God with heart.

Wolves of the spiritual world may encircle mankind, but a Shepherd of old stands alert. Around each follower is an invisible fence ready to send megavolts through any who dare enter the Shepherd's surroundings.

2) *"But God does not take away life; instead, he devises ways so that a banished person may not remain estranged from him"* (2 Samuel 14:14).

The Romans 8:28 of the Old Testament.

The 20th-century chemist looking for a cure for cancer.

The caring professor extending office hours to give a student an opportunity to go from 'D' to 'C'.

The understanding coach, looking for a spot on his roster for the uncoordinated.

The thoughtful employer looking for a place on his payroll for the unhireable.

Were the plans of heaven unveiled for the present five billion to make it to heaven, our individual spreadsheets would contain information that would both humble and inspire us. Never again would we say God did not care. Never again would we question his activity in our lives. The only possible problem in analyzing our spreadsheets might come from attempts to discern certain words—smeared as a result of dropped tears God sheds as you and I refuse one attempt after another to get us home.

1) *"There is no one like the God of Jeshurun, who rides on the heavens to help you and on the clouds in his majesty. The eternal God is your refuge, and underneath are the everlasting arms"* (Deuteronomy 33:26-27).

Nobody has bigger biceps than God. His gymnasium—the world. His workout routine—you and me. We have been carried on a regular basis. With each lift, God gets stronger. Mr. Universe who created it.

God Is Hard-line

10) *"He has showed you, O man, what is good. And what does the LORD require of you? To act justly and to love mercy and to walk humbly with your God"* (Micah 6:8).

Options and suggestions, or requirements and commandments? A God need not suggest. He has earned the right to require.

Yet many in religious circles have hired preachers to point out but not insist. A "come when you want, pray when you need, serve when you think of it, share when you feel like it, give when you can" message that leaves most who hear it lifeless, and all who adhere to it lost.

9) *"The LORD spoke to me with his strong hand upon me, warning me not to follow the way of this people"* (Isaiah 8:11).

The Isaelites had lost what they once had: conviction. Isaiah still had it and was admonished to keep it.

What was "the way" of this people? *Their* way. That was the problem. They had borrowed the old Burger King, "Have It Your Way" slogan for their spiritual lives. They had introduced and were heavily marketing "Cafeteria Christianity"—

go through the line and pick whatever you like. If you don't like it, don't bother.

Religious restaurants are still open today. And God still looks for modern-day Isaiahs who will burn the menu or boycott. Those who long for commands more than compromise. Men and women looking to fulfill the requirements of God and willing to forgo the rituals of man. Committed soldiers who will *do* regardless of how they *feel*.

8) *"That is why the Israelites cannot stand against their enemies; they turn their backs and run because they have been made liable to destruction. I will not be with you anymore unless you destroy whatever among you is devoted to destruction"* (Joshua 7:12).

The God who monitors lifestyle in the 20th century sounds a similar warning for any involved in modern-day activity devoted to destruction.

"I will not be with you anymore unless you get immorality and impurity out of your heart, your life and your church."

"I will not be with you anymore unless you destroy your idols of money, relationships, comfort, television, children or career."

Where did we earn the right to expect everything from God without giving everything to him?

7) *"Aaron's sons Nadab and Abihu took their censers, put fire in them and added incense; and they offered unauthorized fire before the LORD, contrary to his command. So fire came out from the presence of the LORD and consumed them, and they died before the LORD. Moses then said to Aaron, 'This is what the LORD spoke of when he said: 'Among those who approach me I will show myself holy; in the sight of all people I will be honored.' Aaron remained silent"* (Leviticus 10:1-3).

From ordained priests of God performing acts to bring people forgiveness to ordinary people concocting Satanic brew in a cauldron called Compromise.

What prompted this unusual display of fire?

Maybe they were cold and thought God would warm up to the idea.

Maybe they were having some fun, unaware they would soon be fuel.

Perhaps they were out of the correct coals, but thought God would honor quickness as well as quality.

Maybe they were having a bad day. A rebellious day. A little feisty. Feeling a bit like Dennis the Menace only to find out God and Mr. Wilson had nothing in common.

Whatever it was that day that led to the first recorded priestly funeral, God left the Israelites and us a stern warning: DON'T MESS WITH THE RECIPE!

Feelings may be fine, but facts are for sure. Traditions are of man. Truth is of God.

Who are the modern-day Nadabs and Abihus?

Those who involve themselves in all the sexual acts save intercourse and claim to be pure before the Lord.

Self-acclaimed church leaders without biblical backing. They love the position but have yet to earn it.

Part time, three-quarters time and most-of-the-time church-goers who think God only takes attendance on Sundays.

The "I just believe" believers.

The "Pray Jesus into your heart" folks looking for salvation without looking at context.

Those who explain away the clear "baptism for the forgiveness of sin" concept found in the New Testament, clinging to their man-made idea of "an outward sign of inward grace," and "It is important but not necessary."

Smell the fire burning?

God has a keen sense of smell. Who taught us that he doesn't mean what he says? The unauthorized fires burn brightly all over the religious world. God looks for fire fighters willing to work in dangerous territory to put them out. Those looking to uphold his honor by upholding his word.

6) *"Now all has been heard; here is the conclusion of the matter: Fear God and keep his commandments, for this is the whole* *duty of man. For God will bring every deed into judgment, includ-ing every hidden thing, whether it is good or evil"* (Ecclesiastes 12:13-14).

Solomon's swan song. From a man who saw it all, knew it all, felt it all, experienced it all, and had it all, this was all he wanted his readers to remember. Keep the command-ments because *God keeps track.*

Jokes about judgment day abound, but if you are not ready to face the music, you'd better put all jokes aside and get on a serious note.

I never was much for final exams in college. But know-ing some basic guidelines to graduation, I ultimately got down to business, opened my books and tried my best to pull my-self (and my grades) together. It would do all of us good to think about judgment day daily, yet some churches never preach about it, and certainly are not preparing people for it. If it really is the whole duty of man to fear and obey, how many hours are you putting in each week?

5) *"Acquitting the guilty and condemning the innocent–the* LORD *detests them both"* (Proverbs 17:15).

God actually gets an attitude? Most have never even con-ceived that God could detest anything. True, the patience of God does allow him to tolerate beyond human understanding, but the giver of the cross will not be crossed. His truth cannot be confused. When dark is light and light is dark, God intervenes.

Consider the contrasts.

From *"among you there must not be even a hint of any kind of impurity"* (Ephesians 5:3-4) to "as long as we don't have inter-course before marriage we're all right."

From the smoke-filled pages of Sodom and Gomorrah (Genesis 18-19) to "a gay, alternative lifestyle."

From *"honor thy father and mother"* (Ephesians 6:1-3) to a selfish generation looking to nursing homes as the first op-tion, not the last, for their aging parents.

A world turned upside down by Satan that God looks upon with disgust.

4) *"If you fear the Lord and serve and obey him and do not rebel against his commands, and if both you and the king who reigns over you follow the Lord your God–good. But if you do not obey the Lord, and if you rebel against his commands, his hand will be against you, as it was against your fathers"* (1 Samuel 12:14-15).

In case you forgot about the "if" word, this verse will surely jog your memory. God is a God of covenants, offering contracts daily. A mutual agreement between two parties binding one upon the other. You serve, God blesses. You stop, God stops. You follow, God leads. You forget, God leaves.

You work, you get paid. You stop, you get fired. Why is it so easy to understand the truth in the physical world yet miss it in the spiritual realm? Veils.

3) *"Then the Spirit of God came upon Zechariah son of Jehoaida the priest. He stood before the people and said 'This is what God says: "Why do you disobey the Lord's commands? You will not prosper. Because you have forsaken the Lord, he has forsaken you"'"* (2 Chronicles 24:20).

God-moochers. Wanting all God has to offer with no plan for an offering.

All of us have mooched in our lives before and perhaps came away unscathed. Or, maybe we learned all the short-cuts to success only to see success be cut short. Regardless of your mooch success ratio, you always lose when you mooch off of your Maker.

I remember my first year attending Western Washington University, a four-year liberal arts university in Bellingham, Washington, enrolling about 11,000 students. I had attended a junior college near my hometown for two years, then transferred to Western in 1979. I mooched in Junior College. I had the brains (some will disagree) plus a simple schedule, plus the help of my father the math teacher. I received around a 3.5 GPA. The only class I really struggled with was Basic Algebra, but my mooch instincts carried me through, or should I say Dad carried me through. Dad did not come to

Western. As hard as I looked for mooch replacements, I found none.

My first semester journalism law class was said to be challenging, but I figured my intellect would see me through. The 'D' on my midterm, needless to say, brought me to my knees. Humility with a capital 'H' had arrived at my doorstep and without knocking, invited himself in. For the first time, the phrase 'school commitment' entered my vocabulary. Sports commitment—no problem. Girls—no problem (well maybe a few). School—this is new territory. Uncharted territory. Out there by myself with rescue only a remote possibility. I realized then that if I planned to graduate, some study must be involved. Fear helped me a lot. Fear of failure. Fear of my parents' reaction. Fear of 'F'.

The library soon became more than just a place for bookworms and brain donors. Now, silence and bookshelves were not my thing, but neither were 'F's, so I studied and studied. Effort. Late nights. As much as I tried, I found no mooch-holes (similar to loopholes). Just me and my journalism law books.

My final grade: 'A'. 100% on the final. 100 points on my term paper.

Though at the time I did not realize it, God was teaching me in school what he would later teach me in life. If you serve him, he will never leave you. If Mooch is your middle name, and God is your target, hell is what you'll hit.

2) *"Their deeds do not permit them to return to their God. A spirit of prostitution is in their heart; they do not acknowledge the* LORD. *Israel's arrogance testifies against them; the Israelites, even Ephraim, stumble in their sin; Judah also stumbles with them. When they go with their flocks and herds to seek the* LORD, *they will not find him; he has withdrawn himself from them"* (Hosea 5:4-6).

God *will* walk in fellowship with all who sin (1 John 1:7-9)—otherwise he walks with no one. But arrogance and prostitution with the world will stop God in his tracks.

Did you feel something slip away, but decided to keep walking anyway? God probably parked while you proceeded.

Refusing to see and change your sin forces a holy and forgiving God to remove himself from your life. Turn your life around and go back to where you left God standing. He is still there, waiting with an outstretched hand.

1) *"But the LORD said to Moses and Aaron, 'Because you did not trust in me enough to honor me as holy in the sight of the Israelites, you will not bring this community into the land I give them'"* (Numbers 20:12).

Moses had to give up his ticket. The man who had bent over backwards to move God's people forward to Canaan, now takes a giant step backwards. The hard-line prophet of a hard-line God had forgotten to be hard-line.

"Talk to the rock, Moses," commanded God.

But he hit it instead and probably could have hit himself when he did.

"Oops."

The Promise Land was now only available in panoramic view. His feet would never touch the soil. His hands would never pick the golf ball-size grapes. The land of milk and honey was gone.

If Moses, to whom God spoke as a man speaks to his friend, was not an exception, what makes you and me one? God is hard-line with everyone and demands our obedience and our loyalty.

God Is Just

10) *"The LORD detests all the proud of heart. Be sure of this: They will not go unpunished"* (Proverbs 16:5).

My son, Bradley, hopes Dad will forget. Those times in a grocery line or a traffic jam where immediate discipline is not a option, the promise "You will get a spanking when we get home" is hope for him. His only hope is that Dad will forget. It has happened. Not often, though. One time he knew I had forgotten and told me about it when he thought it was safe to do so. He still got his spanking. He has never done that again.

God never forgets. If we don't get our lives in order, punishment is inevitable.

9) *"If in spite of these things you do not accept my correction but continue to be hostile toward me, I myself will be hostile toward you and will afflict you for your sins seven times over'"* (Leviticus 26:23-24).

We like the hundredfold-blessing verses, but few have pitched their tents here to study this verse. Reserved for those who refuse to let the Bible guide their lives and refuse to stop being hostile toward God.

Golf has always been a favorite sport of mine. Especially in college as my roommate and I took advantage of every opportunity to play—and made even more of them. On one May afternoon in 1980, I had developed a serious stomachache. Not enough, of course, to stop a golfaholic. Lightning *and* a stomachache maybe, but not just a stomachache. Driving to the course, I began holding my stomach and questioning my sanity. The golf gods beckoned though, and 75-degree sunny weather in rainy Washington may have been another year in coming, so I toughened up, paid my green fees and headed out to the first tee. It was a busy day on the course so there was some time between each shot to wait for those ahead of us to clear out. I spent more time on the ground lying down than on my feet. Oh, for a golf cart that day! I made two straight pars to open my round but with each hole my stomach problems intensified. Unfortunately, I paid more attention to my putter than my pain, and by God's grace, I am alive to tell about it. Six hours later I had an emergency appendectomy.

I think I shot a 40 (nine holes) that day and the story always gets a great laugh, but life and golf are two different games. Too many refuse the warnings signs, and wrapped up in their own little game, die before they reach the place where they could be helped.

God will punish. God does punish. Accept the correction. Repent of the hostility. God loves rewarding much more than punishing.

8) *"'But you—your bodies will fall in this desert. Your children will be shepherds here for forty years, suffering for your unfaithfulness, until the last of your bodies lies in the desert. For forty years—one year for each of the forty days you explored the land—you will suffer for your sins and know what it is like to have me against you'"* (Numbers 14:32-34).

So much for the idea that God is *for* everybody forever. God stands *against* those who refuse to do right. The Israelites' fear, faithlessness, grumbling and complaining turned God from friend to enemy.

Many live today certain that God is with them, yet have no biblical proof to substantiate their claim. The wrath of God is real. The Israelites felt 40 years of it.

7) *"When a trumpet sounds in a city, do not the people tremble? When disaster comes to a city, has not the* LORD *caused it?"* (Amos 3:6).

Tornadoes—tricks of Mother Nature or tools of God?

Hurricanes—sent from hell to pester mankind temporarily, or sent from heaven so mankind won't be pestered by hell permanently?

Earthquakes—accidental cracks or God's fault?

Wars, famine and daily disasters—God-ordained wake-up calls designed to send panic and pure fear to the living so wrath will be possible only for the dead.

6) *"The* LORD *has opened his arsenal and brought out the weapons of his wrath. For the Sovereign* LORD *Almighty has work to do in the land of the Babylonians"* (Jeremiah 50:25).

Weapons so powerful that the nations once perched atop the charts in world dominance ceased to exist. No nuclear weapons, only a promise of God to destroy and annihilate. The nations who distanced themselves from God and his commandments have long been destroyed. Jericho, Bablyon, Medo-Persia, Greece, Rome, and others—all former champions of the world who found God a foe uncontained.

Only bedtime stories about Jericho and graham-cracker-like walls remain.

The beautiful hanging gardens of Babylon could not hang on. We only trust they once brought wonder to the eyes that gazed upon them.

Persia, now known for cats and rugs, was once touted as an unbeatable foe.

Greece, with its great Alexander bent on conquest, is now only a dream vacation with tours of rubbled ruins.

Rome fiddled around until God broke their every string. Now fountains and an empty Colosseum are a few highlights of the fallen city.

Those who refuse to learn the lesson will realize God's arsenal is never empty. Plentiful weaponry remains to humble each individual and each nation of men who serve themselves and their appetites while ignoring their God.

5) *"For it was the LORD himself who hardened their hearts to wage war against Israel, so that he might destroy them totally, exterminating them without mercy, as the LORD had commanded Moses"* (Joshua 11:20).

God hardens hearts. That is what it says.

God wages war. Do not try to explain it carefully and lovingly.

God destroys. God exterminates without mercy.

You cannot read this passage and feel good. It was not meant to make us feel good. It is there to put fear in our hearts. It is there to give us a complete picture of God. If you bug God and keep on being an oversized pest, extermination is your destiny.

4) *"But those who hate him he will repay to their face by destruction; he will not be slow to repay to their face those who hate him. Therefore, take care to follow the commands, decrees and laws I give you today"* (Deuteronomy 7:10).

What is the "therefore" *there for?* So you won't face the face of anger, the face of wrath.

Why the intensity? Why the livid language? Because there should be absolutely no reason to hate God. Hate the One who made you, molded you, mapped out your life and made provision for your sin?

Those who reach this point have an appointment with God not recorded in their planners but logged securely in the annals of heaven on its final page. The meeting will be short, the sentence long.

3) *"Therefore this is what the Sovereign LORD says, 'My anger and my wrath will be poured out on this place, on man and beast, on the trees of the field and on the fruit of the ground, and it will burn and not be quenched'"* (Jeremiah 7:20).

Sounds harsh until you realize how long God had waited for his people to repent and how he was willing to bless them once they had. These were rebellious people. People *unwilling* to change. God deals in wrath with that type of heart. This wrath would be so furious that man would suffer and everything around him would feel the consequences. Those who lived would, in one sense, be better off dead. God *does* punish those who continue to turn away from him.

2) *"'Who will have pity on you, O Jerusalem? Who will mourn for you? Who will stop to ask how you are? You have rejected me,' declares the LORD. 'You keep on backsliding. So I will lay hands on you and destroy you; I can no longer show compassion. I will winnow them with a winnowing fork at the city gates of the land. I will bring bereavement and destruction on my people, for they have not changed their ways'"* (Jeremiah 15:5-7).

If you read the few verses prior to these strong words of the Almighty, you will see that God had no plans for pardon.

Moses and Samuel had a reputation, not only with man, but with God. These were two of the very few men who had access to the deeper recesses of God's heart. They were there on occasion to turn away his anger from his people and bring mercy one more time. Not this time.

Death was coming without deliverance. God's sword was out of the scabbard bent on destruction. Food was nowhere to be found. Captivity, imprisonment and exile would become like vacation spots for those who survived. No prayer of pardon would reach the Dumbo-sized ears of the One enthroned in heaven. It was as though God had intentionally plugged them as a father would when he grew tired of his teenager's continual playing of loud, but senseless music favorites.

God wishes, wants and works to never see these days arrive. Just don't plan on him wimping out when it comes time to dish out the discipline. God *must* spank a rebellious world, nation or individual. His oversized paddle board is ready to be used daily for those who refuse to change their ways.

1) *"But they mocked God's messengers, despised his words and scoffed at his prophets until the wrath of the Lord was aroused against his people and there was no remedy"* (2 Chronicles 36:16).

Mocked. Despised. Scoffed.

Wrath. Wrath without remedy.

When the sin that causes a cancer-like problem has no chemotherapy to curb it or cure it.

When hope for change was changed to no hope.

When the disease of sin and rebellion forced the angelic apothecary to close its doors.

When God turned his back completely.

When hope died and those who died had no hope.

When pharmaceutical production plummeted and pain prevailed.

When God said No.

God Is Good

10) *"Give thanks to the Lord, for he is good; his love endures forever"* (1 Chronicles 16:34).

If you think enough, you will never be able to thank enough. There is so much good we receive daily from God and so little trouble, yet we still manage to doubt his goodness. Become a person of the good list. Take the time to write down all the good, then all the bad and all your troubles. The good should be as numerous as the Johnsons and Browns in New York City's phone book. The bad, as few as the Kwasnyzalinskis. What number have you been dialing?

9) *"God saw all that he had made, and it was very good"* (Genesis 1:31).

The same feeling you get after a job well done. An artist's masterpiece or an athlete's MVP performance. Much like Michaelangelo upon first sight of the finished Sistine ceiling. Or Julia Child's first bite into her just-out-of-the-oven souffle. Only a good God makes good things. Only a great God makes very good things.

8) *"And now, O Israel, what does the LORD your God ask of you but to fear the LORD your God, to walk in all his ways, to love him, to serve the LORD your God with all your heart and with all your soul, and to observe the LORD's commands and decrees that I am giving you today for your own good?"* (Deuteronomy 10:12-13).

I'm glad God included that last part.

"For your own good."

Take away that life-changing phrase, and God leaves you to fear, walk, obey all, love unconditionally, serve, observe and follow completely. Now, granted, God did not *have to* tell us to do anything that would ultimately help us. He's God, remember. But why do you suppose we have all those commands?

Have you tried flying a kite in Chicago without a string? Splat!

Driven a car in San Francisco without good brakes? Screech, crash!

Seen a child without rules? Trouble.

So, too, a world without the Bible means murders, starvation, divorce, abuse, rape, anger, slander, abortion, death and hell.

7) *"'Bring the whole tithe into the storehouse, that there, may be food in my house. Test me in this,' says the LORD Almighty, 'and see if I will not throw open the floodgates of heaven and pour out so much blessing that you will not have enough room for it.'"* (Malachi 3:10)

For the times you feel like you're doing all the work and God took a vacation. The truth—you give your best, God goes beyond. You obey the simple directions; God gives you a treasure map.

So, life is currently not all that good? First, examine what you are missing; then see why you are missing out. God has never failed any test. You start doing right and watch the finances finally change colors from red to black. But it is not only material blessings that God wants to throw your way. It's the "no price tag presents" that you will never tire of owning. Put God first, and watch lasting friendships come your way. Serve him above all others, and watch joy stay for longer than a needed vacation or a good ball game. Bring him your best effort consistently, then look for hope racing around the nearest corner.

With all the blessings, both physical and spiritual, at God's disposal, there is more than enough for everyone.

6) *"O, Sovereign LORD, you are God! Your words are trustworthy, and you have promised these good things to your servant"* (2 Samuel 7:28).

"Till death do us part" has died.

"I do" most often becomes "I don't."

"Oh, this is the best car on the lot." Spoken daily by lemon legionnaires.

Cards signed "love, always and forever" found at the bottom of disappointment barrels.

"Mom and I aren't getting a divorce. We just need some time away from each other."

The words you trusted completely at 12 now haunt you at 20.

Who can you trust? In a world of lies, broken promises and shattered trust, God's resume should become interesting reading material:

GOD

Address — Everywhere

Current Employment — World and Universal
    Management

Experience — Eternal

Skills — Dead raising, flooding and recovery,
    carpentry, mountain moving, sky writ-
    ing, meteorology, entire city demoli-
    tion and repair, foreign language in-
    structor

Unique qualifications — Friendly, outgoing,
    patient, trustworthy

References — Moses (Former Ambassador to
    Egypt), Solomon (Former President
    of World Gold Market), Jonah
    (Former Sea World Spokesman)

A more-than-impressive God looking to work on your be-
half. Don't take this resume and file it for future reference.

5) *"This only have I found; God made mankind upright, but
men have gone in search of many schemes"* (Ecclesiastes 7:29).

If God is so good, then why are there so many bad people,
and why does evil seemingly prevail?

The God-blamers abound. None of them own mirrors.
It is so easy to blame God. No change will be required if **God**
blew it. Simple, maybe. False, absolutely. God made us for

good because he is good. We have been set up for success but instead go after the schemes. Not content with the garden gala we look for the forbidden fruit. Was God good to Adam and Eve? He allowed the maximum and forbade the minimum. God came with a message to the first couple that has been delivered to every human since: "I am good."

But poisoned fruit still sells cheaply at most corner markets. The vendors—modern day serpents slithering through our lives.

The vendors selling you on selling yourself no matter what the cost—your wife, your kids, your integrity.

The fantasy vendors pointing you to the prostitute on the corner, the pornographic rack on your way and the cybersex on the Internet.

The relationship vendors giving out addresses of local bars and nightclubs and phone numbers of lonely but lustful losers.

The justification vendors selling trash bags full of personal history garbage and the inside scoop on all who have helped ruin your life.

We buy. We buy often. And with each purchase, we slide deeper into the pit of despair, shouting as we go, "God, you put me here!"

Read the verse again and if you are shouting, shut up. If you are just short of the shouting but tempted to listen to others, throw down a copy of Ecclesiastes 7:29 for the sliders, and keep one for yourself.

4) "'*For they have not listened to my words,' declares the* Lord. '*Words that I sent to them again and again by my servants the prophets*'" (Jeremiah 29:19).

One obvious characteristic of a good man is his willingness to persevere with someone of lesser abilities, and at the same time, offer that person assistance. That sounds a lot like what God does for five billion people daily.

How much does God do to help us to make it? We may never know. But I like the phrase "again and again." I would bet if God were flesh and angels became visible, we would be overwhelmed with how often they were hanging around and embarrassed at the number of times we doubted their presence.

But so many of us have gone the route of Gilligan. Continual opportunities arise to get us off the island, but our repeated blunders are preventing it. The islands of loneliness, fear, failure, emptiness and many others are densely populated with spiritual castaways. Many have settled for less and settled in. If you are on that island, then the next boat is for you. God is on it, and there is space available. I recommend you board quickly. Islands have been known to say Hello to hurricanes that say Good-bye to residents.

3) *"This is what your sovereign LORD says, your God who defends his people"* (Isaiah 51:22).

Finally, someone to stick up and speak up for us.

Feeling picked-on? Abused? Mistreated? Wrongly accused? Don't panic, get yourself a good lawyer. A Perry Mason with no need for evidence or a good secretary.

Being stalked? Hire some police protection without badges or beats! The angels in the millions armed to demolish Satan's strongholds, following specific plans of the Great Defender.

God loves to defend us. My son finds folly with the best of them, but when it comes time to defend him against the elements of elementary school, I am there in a heartbeat. If we earthly fathers have that inner intensity to rescue our offspring, definitely count on God to be there when you need him most.

2) *"This is what the LORD your God says—your Redeemer, the Holy One of Israel: 'I am the LORD your God, who teaches what is best for you, who directs you in the way you should go. If only you had paid attention to my commands, your peace would have been like a river, your righteousness like the waves of the sea'"* (Isaiah 48:17-18).

If only you had laid off the liquor, your children would love to spend time with you in your later years.

If only you had disciplined your boy, the probation officer would not be your partner.

If only you had played it safe with your purity, pregnancy could have been reserved for marriage and parenthood shared.

If only you had held your tongue from making all those hurtful and degrading remarks, perhaps your ex-wife would still consider you a great guy, and the divorce damages could have been avoided.

The "if onlys" that need not be. A good God has given us tremendous forewarnings. He teaches. He directs. We learn. We act.

1) *"They will be my people, and I will be their God. I will give them singleness of heart and action, so that they will always fear me for their own good and the good of their children after them. I will make an everlasting covenant with them: I will never stop doing good to them, and I will inspire them to fear me, so that they will never turn away from me. I will rejoice in doing them good and will assuredly plant them in this land with all my heart and soul'"* (Jeremiah 32:38-41).

God is good. He never stops doing good and actually enjoys what he does.

Good cubed to the math majors.

An unassisted triple play to the baseball fan.

The trifecta that came in to the racetrack regulars.

The four-star triple-feature to the movie buff.

If you had three thumbs they would all be pointing up. Good, good, good. What a God!

Long chapter wasn't it? But it needed to be. There is a lot of information about God in the Old Testament that too many have never read. But this is just a sprinkle in the waterfall of truth about our great God. Keep reading. The more you do, the more you know. The more you know, the more you will love the God of the Old Testament.

Chapter Eight

The New

'As for the person who hears my words but does not keep
them, I do not judge him. For I did not come to judge the
world, but to save it. There is a judge for the one who
rejects me and does not accept my words; that very word
which I spoke will condemn him at the last day. For I
did not speak of my own accord, but the Father who sent
me commanded me what to say and how to say it. I know
that his command leads to eternal life. So whatever I say
is just what the Father has told me to say'"
(John 12:47-50).

The New Testament.

Fewer chapters. Fewer verses. Fewer years. Same God.

From the birth of John the Baptist in Galilee to the writings of John the Apostle on Patmos.

From Jesus at 12 in the temple astounding the grown-ups to Jesus with the Twelve in the temple driving out the hypocrites.

Water-walking, wine-making, and weather-altering miracles.

Drops of sweat and blood at Gethsemane to pools of blood at Golgotha.

Prince of Darkness. Prince of Peace.

Hangings. Heroes.

Fishers of fish to fanatics of the faith.

The preaching of Peter. The persecution of Saul.

Angels unlocking prison doors.

Rocks of jealousy hurled at God's new movement.

Paul's "Poseidon Adventures."

Letters to tired disciples and timid evangelists.

Promises of persecution and plans for Christ's comeback.

Heaven. Hell. Rewards. Punishment.

Satan. And of course, God. Let's visit God through passages in the New Testament. The vision of him just gets clearer.

God Is Holy

10) *"When tempted, no one should say, 'God is tempting me.' For God cannot be tempted by evil, nor does he tempt anyone"* (James 1:13).

Something like the late Lawrence Welk being tempted to play acid rock—highly unlikely. But God has never even been tempted to be evil. Now, it would be incredible to have never *done* evil, but to never be *tempted* with evil—wow! We never have to worry that God will decide to do wrong, get grumpy or sign on with Satan.

9) *"'However, the Most High does not live in houses made by men. As the prophet says: "Heaven is my throne and the earth is my footstool. 'What kind of house will you build for me?' says the Lord. 'Or where will my resting place be? Have not my hands made all these things?'"'"* (Acts 7:48-50).

A New Testament reminder of an Old Testament passage—God is huge. The Sears Tower is his toothpick. He rests his invisible feet on Mt. Everest. The Atlantic is his bathtub, the Caribbean his jacuzzi. The sun to him is like a closet light bulb with waning watts. The trees, mere Lincoln Log playthings.

Needless to say, our best houses are not big enough. Neither is the earth. But even though he fills the universe, just get a Bible and open it, along with your heart, and you will find him.

8) *""Our Father in heaven, hallowed be Your name"""* (Matthew 6:9).

A phrase often spoken but seldom adhered to. Little honor for his honor. The Lord's Prayer legacy lives on while respect for the Lord's name dies out.

Despite man's best efforts to defame his name, he remains hallowed. The name introduced to us in the pages of Exodus as the answer to the question Moses asked of his Creator before facing the Pharaoh—"Who shall I say sent me?"

Jehovah God. The great "I AM." He was, is and always will be.

Many names have become hallowed through the years. Plato, Socrates, and Aristotle—philosophers whose wisdom has been kept in most college curricula but who also have both birthdays and tombstones.

Attila, Charlemagne, Alexander, Napoleon and Hitler—military giants who make appearances in all history books but all await the judgment of God based upon their personal history.

Shakespeare, Bryant, Longfellow, Dickens and Hemingway—masters of the pen with words to inspire, charm and intrigue those who live years later. They offer optional words that pale in comparison to the commandments of the Creator.

Lincoln, Washington, Franklin, Jefferson, King and Kennedy—American heroes whose holidays we enjoy but whose graves we visit.

Only one name will never be etched on an epitaph—God.

7) *"For God is not a God of disorder but of peace"* (1 Corinthians 14:33).

In Corinth, the first-century disciples were operating their church services as though they were merely religious orgies. Wild and crazy worship reigned without order or substance leading to havoc then, hell later. Worldliness had crept into the church, and Paul reminded the disciples of God's true nature—commanding them to settle down. Too many visitors to the church in Corinth and members alike were leaving the assembly confused and closed-hearted and leaving their calendars open for the following Sunday.

No wonder Satan orchestrates confusion. Make a decision to quit the band.

6) *"But do not forget this one thing, dear friends: With the Lord a day is like a thousand years, and a thousand years are like a day"* (2 Peter 3:8).

The first-century Christians expected the return of Jesus yesterday. They quickly began to feel that God had broken his promise to send him back. But God had other plans in mind. The timetables were different shapes and sizes. God sees on an eternal scale while we see with our calendars, daytimers and planners. But it's good to know that the measly amount I can attempt in 24 hours, God has 1,000 years to fix whatever I messed up, finish what I could not, and finalize what I will do tomorrow.

God owns no alarm clocks, needs no wake-up calls, and no calendars hang in his heavenly kitchen. He feels no pressures from deadlines, feels no guilt from missed appointments, and never has cancellations. God experiences none of the whelms, overwhelms or constraints that time has placed upon mankind.

The God outside of time who instituted time so we would have time to make time to follow him through and beyond time.

5) *"...a faith and knowledge resting on the hope of eternal life, which God, who does not lie, promised before the beginning of time..."* (Titus 1:2).

In a world of lies, broken promises and typically dishonored "I swear to God"s, God's honesty and track record are impeccable and appealing. If it is in the Bible, it has happened, is happening, or will happen.

A dark world full of white lies desperately needs a totally truthful God. Man cheats on his wife, his taxes, his neighbor and cheats himself out of a good life, a clear conscience and eternal life. God never lies, never cheats. You may not be able to trust your boss, your spouse, your neighbor or yourself, but God longs for you to look at his unblemished record and put your trust in him.

4) *"The God who made the world and everything in it is the Lord of heaven and earth and does not live in temples built by hands. And he is not served by human hands, as if he needed anything, because he himself gives all men life and breath and everything else"* (Acts 17:25).

Imagine not needing anything. God does not imagine it, he lives it.

He is never thirsty. The Nestea plunge does not excite him. God has no lips to be cracked. The Creator does not get cottonmouth.

He is never hungry. New York steak and baked potato means as much to God as cockroach stew means to you and me.

He is never tired. God stays up all night without caffeine. He never needs a catnap or a power nap. No bedtime or curfew.

Never cold. Never hot. No need for central air in heaven. No thermostats. No insulation. No roof. No home. No nothing.

God is never lonely. He does not need a lended ear or a shoulder to cry on. No hugs are essential to remain secure. No need for smiles or group therapy.

He is never flustered. No need for a vacation or a short break. No need for time to get away from all the pressures of life.

And what about you and me?

Thirsty? Regularly.

Hungry? Even fast food drive-thrus are too slow when the stomach rumbles. More than a minute in the microwave messes me up.

Tired? The morning mattress demons give me regular hugs.

Cold? The Windy City in December may not affect God, but I'm putting on longjohns, two pairs of pants, a hat and earmuffs. And then, if I have to, I'll step outside.

Hot? I tried to tolerate Midwest humidity without a car air-conditioner for three years. I purchased the car in Denver where humidity is heavenly (virtually none), but six months later I was languishing in Lincoln, Nebraska. Seven months later I cooked in Cincinnati, and two years later Chicago offers no relief. I need air-conditioning. I finally acknowledged my "ungodlikeness" and my latest automobile is equipped with proof of my humanity.

I need a house. I need a roof. I would like central-air, central-heat, central everything.

Lonely? Occasionally. Even we men need a lended ear. And, if we were honest, we would look for the lobes a lot more.

Hugs? Good to know from the tight hold that your relationships are holding tight.

Flustered? Only when things are not going as expected. Losing my keys is equal to losing my mind—or is it the other way around?

We need so much. God needs nothing. He is holy.

3) *"Now to the King eternal, immortal, invisible, the only God, be honor and glory for ever and ever. Amen"* (1 Timothy 1:17).

He is King, we are the slaves. He is eternal, we head to the graves. He is immortal, we sin and need to be saved. He is invisible, we are flesh, and flesh we will stay.

He is the only God while we share headlines with five billion plus, all of us acting as though we want his position, but proving to be highly unqualified.

2) *"Oh the depths of the riches of the wisdom and knowledge of God! How unsearchable his judgments and his paths beyond tracing out! 'Who has known the mind of the Lord? Or who has been* *his counselor?' 'Who has ever given to God that God should repay him?' For from him and through him and to him are all things. To him be the glory forever. Amen"* (Romans 11:33-36).

All of us have achieved most of our successes with the help and input of others. Little, if anything, we have discovered by ourselves. We have been taught everything.

But God never seeks advice. Who could offer a better way? Who would dare try? Who can teach God anything?

How about some basketball lessons? He placed huge spheres in exactly the right places. Don't tell me he can't shoot hoops.

Bowling? The unshakeable walls of Jericho fell with men marching and horn blowing. Ten pins are not a stiff challenge to him.

Cooking? We take a rib from a single cow and make a meal. God took a rib from a single man and made a marriage partner.

God does not need the couch, he is not working on overcoming, and he purchases no "self-help" books. How smart is God? We may never know. How deep is his wisdom? Way over our heads!

1) *"God, the blessed and only Ruler, the King of kings and Lord of lords, who alone is immortal and who lives in unapproachable light, whom no one has seen or can see. To him be honor and might forever. Amen"* (1 Timothy 6:15-16).

The occupant of the House of Lights. We dare not try to get in.

I have always been fascinated with beautiful houses, those million-dollar mansions made with man's most creative design genius. The home says a lot about who lives on the inside. Yet no home is burglar proof, fireproof, waterproof, or windproof. The proof is in the daily newspaper as homes regularly go up in smoke and down the river.

God has no home owner's insurance. He lives in unapproachable light and will never be bothered. So the next time you feel holy and special, take a long look at the sun at

2:00 p.m. and remember that God's residence is ever more radiant. Better yet, put on your most powerful sunglasses, take a glancing look, and get down on your knees to praise the one and only God. Save your eyes the pain today, and save your soul the pain forever.

God Is Powerful

10) *"For God did not give us a spirit of timidity, but a spirit of power, of love and of self-discipline"* (2 Timothy 1:7).

While most of us tackle timidity problems regularly, God has never been one to struggle with being shy. He was not afraid to confront Adam and Eve after their inaugural sins and was quick to call Cain in on murder charges. He gave Moses the confidence needed to face the Pharaoh and demand a permanent vacation from slavery for him and his people.

Typically, timidity stems not from fear of failure but from fear of what others will *think* of us after we have failed. God is beyond both. He took a killer of Christians and turned him into their worldwide leader. He chose fishermen over etiquette experts to change the world. He made Nebuchadnezzar cuddle up with the cows when everyone else was too afraid to check his pride. He humbled the Herods, and he brought the unbeatable Roman empire to its knees when it refused to kneel before him.

9) *"Why should any of you consider it incredible that God raises the dead?"* (Acts 26:8).

What's the big deal? That's exactly what Paul was trying to communicate to King Agrippa and his welcomed guests in one of his many defenses of being a follower of the resurrected Christ.

Daily, thousands of babies are conceived. "No problem," we say. And, though many of us lack the scientific insight to explain this process (other than it is fun), we have no problem seeing that it works. But what is more amazing? God giving life back to something that once had it but lost it, or God giving life to something that never had it? I say the latter.

If God made Adam from the dust, then he can take the dead bones of decayed bodies and dusty remains of you and me and put us back together for eternity. If God made you and me from an egg and a sperm and formed us over nine months in our mother's womb, I see no problem believing that Jesus is now alive, and death is only temporary for us all. But the fact remains that both coming to life and coming back to life are pretty incredible. Only if you're not God.

8) *"But if it is from God, you will not be able to stop these men; you will only find yourselves fighting against God"* (Acts 5:39).

Spoken by a non-disciple to convince the first-century enemies of the cross they need to cool off before they get cooked.

There are a few things in our world that you would do well to not mess with. Barbed wire is one that comes to my mind. Daily I am reminded of my weakness as I look in the mirror and see scars on my face, neck, arms and all the way down the right side of my body. The scars of my humanity are a result of the simple equation: Motorcycle + Inexperience + Barbed Wire = Pain. (Stupidity could be in there, but the scars are painful enough without admitting how stupid it was.)

I was 13 at the time and visiting my best friend, Randy Daggy, in Chehalis, Washington. It was a hot summer day, and we were about 15 minutes from a nice, cool dip in the nearby Chehalis River. I had on shorts and a t-shirt (the shirt would have been off, but remember *the hole*), great swimwear, but not what I would have chosen had I seen the barbed wire coming in my near future. Randy decided to take a quick spin around the farm on a mini-bike he owned. I was apprehensive to ride due to my fear of motorcycles after my brother's death, so I decided to abstain. But it looked like so much fun. And, after all, it wasn't like I would be riding a

Harley-Davidson. I thought, "I can do this." And I did. I took my first lap with confidence, building up speed as I went. As I headed toward the home stretch, something from deep within told me to take a victory lap. (I know now there are such things as motorcycle demons.)

My victory lap started off innocently. I now was an experienced rider, thus accelerating at every opportunity and turning corners at sharper angles. And, though I could see the fence of doom looming on the horizon, I was still okay. Just slow down a bit, stop if necessary, turn the steering mechanism, and the barbed wire will still only be used to keep in the cows. I did all of that except, in a panic, or another one of my "brain-dead" moments, while reaching for the brake, grabbed the accelerator, sped up and headed straight into the jagged edges of wire. I was no match. Though I was going about 25-30 m.p.h. (it seemed like 90), I stopped. The fence had won. I was not going through, and I would pay dearly for even trying.

More than 100 stitches and permanent scars have taught me a few painful yet valuable lessons of life. Humans should not mess with barbed wire. Cats should not start fights with canines. Createds should not challenge creators.

Stop fighting God. Regardless of how big you think your motorcycle is, God rides on the clouds.

7) *"I tell you that out of these stones God can raise up children for Abraham"* (Matthew 3:9).

The words of John the Baptist to the prideful, elitist Jews who thought they had a lock on God because of birthright. A few years later, when told to keep his people quiet upon his donkey ride into Jerusalem, Jesus proclaimed that rocks would cry out in jubilation if need be (Luke 19:28-40).

Talking rocks. Laughing rocks. Crying rocks. The closest we get to these are pet rocks. But God can take a rock and really make it your pet. If he did it from dust, seems to me a rock would not be any more difficult.

Mt. Rushmore is man's creation. Imagine the tourist trap it would become if God took those ex-chiefs of state, brought them to life and made them talk. The next time you see a rock, consider the power it took to make it, then imagine that your next-door neighbor used to be one. God could do it, you know. We throw them, skip them, crush them, decorate with them, kick them (only the small ones if you're smart), climb them and paint them with graffiti. We have yet to decipher how to make them breathe.

6) *"Jesus looked at them and said, 'With man this is impossible, but with God all things are possible'"* (Matthew 19:26).

Open wide your imagination with this one, and stop limiting God.

The sun could disappear and we could still live!

A baby could speak eloquently at birth.

Barking birds. Purring puppies. Cats that chirp.

Now, I am not a frequent visitor to the *National Enquirer* rack myself, but as outlandish as some of those headline stories seem, God would have no problem making any of them happen. Maybe the birth of Isaac would have been tabloid material in early days.

"Ninety-Year-Old Mom Seen in Delivery Room at Local Hospital." (see photos inside)

Which soap opera did you see that on?

"Walls of Jericho Collapse."

"The reporter must have collapsed first."

"I would have to see it to believe it."

"You sure that wasn't in California along the fault line?"

"Red Sea Parts."

"The reporters must be on drugs."

"I'll wisely pass by that one."

"Let's buy *Egypt Today* and get the real facts."

"Man Last Seen Heading for Heaven in Chariot of Fire."

"It was just an unusual cloud configuration."

"That is way too sensational to sell."

"Somebody must have been burning trash in the area."

"Fiery Furnace Produces No Burns on the Boys."

"Oh, it's just that illusionist's deception again. Wasn't Shadrach's last name Houdini, or something like that?"

"Lions Lay Low With Babylonian Troublemaker—They Sleep While He Pets."

"Daniel must have been a lion-tamer on the side."

"Surely he had a huge whip in there with him."

We have become so humanistic we have a hard time believing God can cure cancer, stop starvation or change our children. We search for scientific and sensible explanations for everything. Throw away your test tubes, and open your imagination for a moment, and let's deal with where you are at right now.

"Can my marriage be great?"

All things.

"Can I overcome my past?"

All things.

"Can I get out of debt?"

All things.

"Can I become a leader in my church?"

All things.

"Can I can be happy consistently?"

All things.

"Can I help others to learn about and then follow God?"

All things.

My parents and I *can* be close. My kids *can* learn to love God. I *can* stop drinking. I *can* stop smoking. I *can* stop worrying. I *can* get a good job. I *can* get good grades.

All things. All things. All things. All things.

5) *"For since the creation of the world, God's invisible qualities—his eternal power and divine nature—have been clearly seen, being understood from what has been made, so that men are without excuse"* (Romans 1:20).

How powerful is God? Look. Look some more. The creation is all you need to be convinced that we have a God, and that he is all-powerful.

Take a long look at the bright, blue sky. What can it teach you about God? How about a tree? Learn anything? The sun? That's an easy one. One star (remember there are billions)? A rose? You can even *smell* the power of God. The ocean. The sand. The seashells. The whale. The shark. A waterfall. A river. A man. A woman. A baby.

If you have lost touch with the power of God, get your boots on, take a hike, and go see God. Bring your sleeping bag and count the stars at night if you can. Listen to the creation mingle at night and sing in the morning. Watch the sun come up and describe the reds and yellows. Then pack up your things and come on home. Kiss your wife, hug your kids, take out your baby book, and get perspective. The world is here because of God. You are here because of God. It took power to get us here and takes power to keep us here.

We have no excuse. We and billions more see it daily. But only a few honor him for it and look for that same power to change their average lives into awesome ones. Be one of the few.

4) *"As it is written: 'I have made you a father of many nations.' He is our father in the sight of God, in whom he believed— the God who gives life to the dead and calls things that are not as though they were"* (Romans 4:17).

Imagine the day Abraham and Sarah walked into the Mesopotamia Medical Center, sat down with the top-notch doctors, and sought out medical advice on how this "baby thing" was going to come about. Having sought out adoption alternatives that were nixed by God, and after an attempt to bring junior through a much younger and abler childbearer, Abraham and Sarah concluded that God was not just pulling their leg. He really wanted 99-year-old Abraham and 90-year-old Sarah to reproduce.

"But what will all those youngsters in Lamaze class think? Will they laugh and check for the pillow under the shirt trick?"

"Okay, where is Allen Funt and *Candid Camera*? Who set us up for this practical joke?"

Who would go buy the baby food this week and tell the checker it was not for your grandson's child but yours?

Would they want to include themselves in the family portrait?

Who would coach Isaac's baseball team? Dad can barely breathe, let alone pitch batting practice and hit infield. He would probably die of a heart attack during the first close play at home plate.

What other parents would they hang with?

Good questions that all the doctors at MMC (remember Mesopotamia Medical Center) said were valid "...if something like that could ever happen, which it won't, so go home get your rest, and be content with no kids, and enjoy the rest of your retirement."

But when the harps played perfectly and the sun softly set and Abraham's desire for his wife matched his belief in an all-powerful God, he dragged his good-as-dead body out of his recliner, headed for bed, obeyed the only command that has never been complained about, and got fruitful and multiplied.

If God wants something done and has people willing to be used by him to do it, bag the X-rays, scientific evidence, and the "It's never been done before" excuses, and stand back and be amazed at the power of God. Every cry of Isaac in the middle of the night, every feeding time, every time Abraham stood over his son at night and watched him sleep peacefully, he was reminded that the voice that told him where to go and what to do had power-packed credentials.

The story is there not just for old-timers but for all who struggle with believing in an all-powerful God. So the next time you feel yourself starting to doubt, memorize one word—Isaac. And if need be, consider it seriously before naming your next child.

3) *"By faith we understand that the universe was formed at God's command so that what is seen was not made out of what was visible"* (Hebrews 11:3).

It takes incredible ability to create such masterpieces as the "Mona Lisa" and the "Last Supper." But doggone it, Leonardo had paint. And I'm fairly sure he used a brush, too. God paints without either.

All of us are undoubtedly impressed with the Sears Tower, the Statue of Liberty, and other skyscraper phenoms. But steel, bulldozers, scaffolds, hammers, cranes, work crews, months and years were involved. Mt. Everest arrived simply because God told it to.

So you have never been a confident person, ever in your life? So?

Never been able to make friends? So?

Never had a good marriage? So-o-o-o-o-o-o-o?

God just needs you to believe it can be done. If God made something out of nothing in the creation for our benefit, how much more will he desire to make something out of nothing in our lives. All you have to be is the easel. God has the paint and brush in hand eager to turn you into a masterpiece that you will never want to sell.

2) *"For the foolishness of God is wiser than man's wisdom, and the weakness of God is stronger than man's strength"* (1 Corinthians 1:25).

Got any answers for how we can help people get along? How can we convince leaders of nations to build bridges, not bombs. How can real peace become a real possibility? Should we combine the intellects of the greatest scholars, inventors, scientists, doctors, philosophers and politicians and have them ponder, then put together a world-peace proposal? Or, do we get humans one-by-one to understand the personal implications of the death of a 33-year-old Jewish carpenter on a cross, see their sin, appreciate their forgiveness and slowly but surely tear down the high walls of hostility?

How can we keep people's countenances up while keeping the crime rate down? Should we separate all races, colors, religions, opinions, intelligence levels and economic levels and let them try to enjoy only those of their kind? Or, do we start a church, invite anybody and everybody to come, let them work together, learn from each other, forgive each other and enjoy their diversity?

God's wisdom and his ways have always worked.

E = mc² came about by the Almighty, not Albert. And probably on a bad day, if God ever had one. A man on the moon is no big deal to a God who made both out of nothing. The combined rippling muscles of heavyweight powerlifters, wrestling stalwarts and football middle linebackers throughout the years are comparable to a sprained pinky on the hand of God. We are not in the same league, ballpark or general vicinity. We are outsmarted and outnumbered by one all-powerful God.

1) *"Now to him who is able to do immeasurably more than all we ask or imagine, according to his power that is at work within us, to him be glory in the church and in Christ Jesus throughout all generations, for ever and ever. Amen"* (Ephesians 3:20-21).

Read it again. Did you get that? Introducing Santa Claus all over again, only this time our belief in the Generous One will not need to be temporary.

Santa Claus—the smiling, friendly one who chooses to climb down every chimney as he sweeps across the globe to bring children joy. Do you believe we used to believe that stuff? So naive. So hopeful. So pure. Oh, to be a kid again and exchange Santa Claus for the real thing.

What would you have on your list? What "outlandish" present would you ask for? Why don't you hop up on his lap, put your arms around him, and tell him what you want? Who said dreams don't come true? Who said you have too wild an imagination? Who taught you to limit God?

The sleigh is airborne 24 hours a day, 365 days a year. Put out the fire and the milk and cookies and expect a visit from the One who really can deliver the goods.

God Is Caring

10) *"But love your enemies, do good to them and lend to them without expecting to get anything back. Then your reward will be great, and you will be sons of the Most High, because he is kind to the ungrateful and wicked'"* (Luke 6:35).

How many times have you fit these descriptions?

Ungrateful? God still blesses.

Wicked? God loves to forgive the messes.

How caring is God? He cares for those who do not. He is kind to those who are not. Only God could find mercy for the mass-murderer. Only a loving God would protect Cain from physical harm when he was so deserving of punishment. Only a caring God could allow an adulterer to live on in hopes of being forgiven and becoming faithful once again. Only God could keep himself from picking up the rocks of retaliation ready to destroy the guilty party and, instead, go gather the wood for his Son's cross.

You get the picture. God is so unique. So kind. So considerate. So caring. So unlike us.

9) *"But God has combined the members of the body and has given greater honor to the parts that lacked it"* (1 Corinthians 12:24).

The statistician suddenly becomes more important than the star halfback.

The cymbal's player in the band gets rave reviews for his contributions to the "Star-Spangled Banner."

The garbage collector gets a million-dollar, five-year, no-cut contract.

God has always hovered over the lesser-knowns. Do you feel weak? Look around. Ahead of you is God to protect, behind you is God to push, and beside you is God to pamper. You never again have to feel like a nobody. God champions the cause of the weak and less fortunate. Those we despise, God takes out on a date. Those we avoid, God surrounds.

God's health club membership list is full of the 98-pound weaklings and the tremendously overweight. Too embarrassed to go elsewhere, they know God won't laugh.

God's university is attended by many C+ (at best) students, trying their hardest but something is just not clicking. They all make the dean's list.

God's team. Those that can't dribble, shoot, pass or play defense, but love the exercise and competition. No score is ever kept.

God's church is for everybody.

So you can't speak too well? How many can give a sermon at one time anyway?

Don't have a whole lot of money? How much do you think God has?

Shy? So was Timothy.

No talent? God will help you find some.

Only a caring God can make everybody feel welcomed.

8) *"Or do you show contempt for the riches of his kindness, tolerance and patience, not realizing that God's kindness leads you toward repentance?"* (Romans 2:4).

Sometimes it is the soft, yet powerful, voice of God that changes a wicked and selfish heart. All it took for me one night was five words— "Would you be my pony?"

It was 1990 in Denver, Colorado, and one Saturday I was preparing a sermon I would be preaching the following day. I didn't get too many opportunities to speak to the entire church, so I was a bit nervous. I had not totally decided on a topic but was leaning toward something on servanthood or being others-focused. I was becoming somewhat flustered trying to come up with an outline when my four-year-old asked, "Daddy, would you be my pony?"

"Not right now," I said, meaning, "Ask me one hour from now." But to a child "Not right now" means wait 30 seconds, then ask again. And he did. I raised my voice slightly and repeated, "Not right now." Just 30 seconds later I would receive the rebuke of a lifetime. Not lightning, loud voices or finger pointing, but the tears of a four year-old.

"Daddy, would you be my pony?"

I dropped my pen and shouted, "Bradley, not right now!" He began to cry, and I began to realize what a hypocrite I was. There I was preparing a sermon on living for others, and I would not even be a horse for my own kid. My boy needed a ride. He needed his dad. His dad needed to repent. I did. I got down on all fours and gave him the ride of his life. Not only that, but I had my sermon title for the following day.

When I announced the title, "Would You Be My Pony?" everyone thought I had lost my mind and, with it, any chance of preaching again. All were hoping the sermon would improve upon the title. They got it eventually. I got it too. I got loved by a caring God who helped me to repent through his kindness in showing me my son's tears and then allowing me to become a bucking bronco.

7) *"What then shall we say in response to this? If God is for us, who can be against us? He who did not spare his own Son but gave him up for us all–how will he not also, along with him, graciously give us all things?"* (Romans 8:31-32).

Would God, who decided to let his Son die for you when you essentially could have cared less, not give you all that you need now that you care a lot more? Could a God who forgave you of 30 years of sin and stupidity not care enough to get you out of your most recent bind?

So, you find yourself up against a wall? Is everybody against you? Outnumbered? Five against one? Look again. At least five more angels are somewhere. One thousand to one? God sends a legion. A million to one? God opens the heavens and gives all angels a two-week vacation. They will spend it with you.

6) *"Praise be to the God and Father of our Lord Jesus Christ, the Father of compassion and the God of all comfort"* (2 Corinthians 1:3).

The "all" before the "comfort" is there because we all tend to make ourselves the exception.

"Oh, God can help *them*, but he can't help *me*."

"God can comfort me in *almost* everything."

"I can never overcome *this* depression."

"This loss is devastating. I will never be the same again."

All. All. All.

Divorce discomfort.

"I swear I will never get married again; it's just too difficult."

Parental pain.

"I have done all I can, and my son still doesn't show any signs of getting serious about God."

"We have spanked, ordered tons of time-out's, and grounded regularly, but our daughter is still rebellious."

Loss of loved ones.

"I don't think I can go on; the memories are too painful."

Whenever you get tempted to make yourself the exception, this verse would be an exceptional one to have memorized.

5) *"This is good, and pleases God our Savior, who wants all men to be saved and to come to a knowledge of the truth"* (1 Timothy 2:3-4).

There's that word again. *All*, not some. All. Not most. All. Not an overwhelming percentage. All. And you are included in that *all*. So was Jeffrey Dahmer, the convicted murderer of 17 young men in gruesome, hard-to-forget fashion, who was recently murdered in a Wisconsin prison.

When I first heard the news of his horrendous crimes, I was angry. I still am. But I found reason to care for Jeffrey. While living in Cincinnati, his brother Dave became one of my best friends. Dave is a tremendous man of God, having been a faithful follower for more than seven years. I began to care for Jeffrey because I knew Dave cared for Jeffrey.

When Dave asked me to share a few of my thoughts at Jeffrey's memorial service, quite frankly it was one of the most challenging and scary things I had ever been faced with. Did Jeffrey really have a true conversion before his death?

Was he really going to heaven, even after all the pain he had caused and still causes for so many innocent victims? The question is still unanswered in my mind. But the question of "Could he be forgiven?" is not. Read your Bible if you doubt. All I know is that if the above verse is true, God definitely wanted him to be.

How about a crooked politician? A Mafia main-man? A prostitute? A rapist? A child-abuser? Don't stop caring for those for whom God cares. If they are still alive, so is the chance for forgiveness.

4) *"For surely it is not angels he helps, but Abraham's descendants"* (Hebrews 2:16).

Good news. That's you. Me. Mom. Dad. Son. Daughter.

Angels shouldn't need very much help anyway. They don't have the temptations that come with flesh and bone. They have no space problems. No problems to encounter in knowing the real God. The singing is always as good as the preaching. Food? Always delicious. An exciting purpose to live for? They get to help us knuckleheads and have continual access to a good laugh.

But imagine this: You get priority over an angel. Michael the Archangel gets nothing like the treatment *Michaels* of the world get. Gabes of the world rejoice! (Hopefully nobody named their kid Lucifer.)

God undoubtedly cares for the angels, but humans he cares for *and* helps. What angel did God ever give the perfect woman to marry? What angel ever got the greatest job? What angel did God help escape from sin? What angel did Jesus die for? Angels make it without the help. Certainly we can make it *with* the help!

3) *"Cast all your anxiety on him because he cares for you"* (1 Peter 5:6-7).

There will always be one very simple rule of fishing: you don't cast, you don't catch. The same, simple rule is taught by God. You don't cast, you don't catch. You don't catch answers. You don't catch relief. You don't catch the drift that God really cares. You keep your problems. You keep your anxiety. You keep your high blood pressure. You keep your fits of rage. You keep your fears. You keep on being the same.

The only way to really know how much God cares is to start casting. Cast your job, your marriage, your kids, your schedule, your commitment, your vacations, your sin, your everything on God. Let him prove once and for all how much he cares.

2) *"Are not two sparrows sold for a penny? Yet not one of them will fall to the ground apart from the will of your Father. And even the very hairs of your head are all numbered. So don't be afraid; you are worth more than many sparrows'"* (Matthew 10:29-31).

This is very exciting news to me because I personally cannot stand sparrows. They have ruined many good walks in the park and too many potentially good shots on the golf course. But God actually likes sparrows. He cares for sparrows. Certainly I would not have the audacity to lower myself before a member of the animal kingdom? An eagle maybe. But a sparrow? And my hairs are all numbered. Wow. My Bible even proves that God can subtract. God takes time even for the unimportant. (I wish *I* could say it were unimportant; all things become much more important when you start losing them!)

Now if God cares for my hair, certainly he must be protecting my heart and my health. If God serves lunch to the sparrows, certainly he can keep food on my dinner table. If birds are a big deal, certainly my boy must be. If hairs are numbered, probably my days are as well. If birds don't die outside the will of God, certainly people wouldn't. Would they? Read it again, and stop doubting.

1) *"And we know that in all things God works for the good of those who love him, who have been called according to his purpose"* (Romans 8:28).

How much does God care? So caring he works overtime in the "changing bad to good" business. He works to iron out your wrinkles and mend your messes.

Lost your job? Thought about the possibility of a better one? Maybe *you* blew it. Maybe you were unfairly fired. It doesn't really matter. The verse is still true.

Been sick lately? Maybe you will begin to see how much you are loved. Maybe you will finally find out just how tough you are.

Bad relationship? Maybe you will work much harder at the next one.

Bad marriage? Maybe it will humble you and bring you to God.

Death? Maybe you will appreciate life more, and start making an impact.

It started out a beautiful, snowy Christmas night in Boulder, Colorado, in 1989. The snow in the Rocky Mountains had just begun to descend upon Boulder, and Patty and I were relaxing in our apartment, wondering if we would be able to open the present that day we really wanted—our second child. I could not remember when I had been more excited.

Crib? Check. Diapers? Check. Shower gifts? Check. Lamaze classes? Check. Excitement? Check. Hope? Check.

The call came that night. It was time to go to officially introduce ourselves to the little one God had been hanging with for nine months. We were so calm. (It is usually a lot easier on the second one, isn't it?) We even stopped for gas. I told the attendant we were going to the hospital to have our baby. He wished us the best, and we were on our way to Denver to deliver. Thirty minutes later we casually checked in and went to the birthing room. All the monitors were set. Smiling nurses were all in place. All the paperwork was done. Only hours from now we would have our dream—part two.

"Is the monitor not working, or what?"

"What is going on here?"

"What do you mean, you can't find a heartbeat?"

"Not our baby."

"Do another test. Do an ultrasound."

It was too late, and we knew it. The final ultrasound test only confirmed what was our greatest fear. We would not be taking our baby home, instead we would bury her. She was a girl. We had now completed the perfect, All-American family. There was only one problem. She was dead.

We named her. We held her. We cried over her. We agonized. We agonized some more. We still weep. We still agonize. We still remember our little Melissa.

But five years removed, I see the truth of Romans 8:28 so clearly. I became a better parent to Bradley. I started disciplining him much more consistently and effectively. I lost my daughter to death, I was not about to lose my son to the world. I got completely cared-for by the church in Denver like never before by an outpouring of love and letters until laughter could return.

Fifteen months later, God brought Brittany into our lives. Oh, we were afraid for most of the pregnancy period that something similar would happen. But God knew that. Brittany is five years old now, beautiful and completely healthy. She and I love to snuggle in our favorite chair and call each other "best friends." I had always dreamed of a little girl. I just didn't realize that prior pain would be involved.

I believe that through it all, I am a better man. I have learned to trust. I have learned to fight to find the positive. I now counsel others who have gone through similar tragedies. I am a lot more sensitive. I am a better leader.

Would I have done it another way? Absolutely! But that is why there is only one God. And I know from this powerful verse that this one God really does care.

God Is Hard Line

10) *"Religion that God our Father accepts as pure and faultless is this: to look after orphans and widows in their distress and to keep oneself from being polluted by the world"* (James 1:27).

Contrary to popular opinion, God does not accept every religion.

Some spend countless hours with orphans and widows only to come home to the bottle, a *Playboy* magazine or a rotten marriage. Unacceptable!

Some stay so far away from worldliness they do not see *any* faces, let alone the lonely faces of an orphan or a widow—those who have never smoked, gotten drunk, swore, committed adultery or murdered anyone but remain spiritual couch potatoes, living by themselves and for themselves. Unacceptable!

Some sound the trumpet of orphanage donations, widow's banquets and hospital visitation and think their good deeds cover over their bad behavior. Unacceptable!

True religion—being like Jesus—involves both. You watch your life, say No to the world, and help the hurting in the meantime.

Many, though, may be pleased to hear that God, too, has a bitter disgust with many religions. Either you have his or you have none at all.

9) *"God opposes the proud but gives grace to the humble"* (1 Peter 5:5).

Isn't it great that we get to choose how we will be treated by God? Great only if we choose to be humble. But if you don't get some help on your pride and, with it, some conviction about changing, you are in for a hard life. You will be opposed.

Too many think they can run the show but never show any thanks. Too many think they can climb the ladder of success or climb in bed with anyone and still climb the ladder to heaven. Both are impossible.

God has opposed the greatest. He showed Adam and Eve he meant business during the fruit controversy (Genesis 3). Sweat and labor pains were reminders that God opposes the proud. He burned entire cities filled with those proud of their homosexual lifestyles (Genesis 18-19). He gave Pharaoh nine strong warnings before he took his most treasured possession (Exodus 5-12).

The spear in Saul's gut (1 Samuel 31).

The dead baby in David's nursery (2 Samuel 12).

It was whale innards for Jonah (Jonah 1-2).

Cow company for Nebuchadnezzar (Daniel 4).

Dogs licked up prideful Jezebel's blood (2 Kings 9).

Phineas' spear pierced the unmarried but sexually active Israelite couple (Numbers 25).

All object lessons on the opposition of God.

Those lessons were written down long ago for the 20th-century pride-bearer. Yet, still, today, crooked CEOs and politicians talk of God and hope of heaven. Homosexuals flaunt their sin and demand to be accepted into life's mainstream as well as into church leadership. Unmarried couples live together, sleep together, and go to church together, accepted in many circles as true believers, but shut out of the true circle of God-honorers.

Humble yourself and vow to let *God* run your life. Do not enter the ring with God. You will lose eventually.

8) *"And when you stand praying, if you hold anything against anyone, forgive him, so that you Father in heaven may forgive you your sins"* (Mark 11:25).

Sounds hard line to me, yet simple as well—give and you will get.

"I just cannot forgive Mom for what she did."

"I guess all my bitterness and resentment will be worked out in heaven."

"My ex really messed me up, and I do not think I can ever forgive that."

If your inner thoughts are sounding somewhat similar, then plan on your sins remaining on the heavenly chalkboard while God patiently waits, eraser in hand. God waits to forgive, but you are waiting for the perfect apology.

God says No to a world who campaigns for compassion but offers none. No to a world who hopes for heaven but helps nobody to get there. No to the sons and daughters who refuse to let Mom and Dad back into their lives due to the chaos of childhood. No to the Moms and Dads suffering from past embarrassments who refuse to be parents to the prodigal attempting to find his way home.

7) *"For if you forgive men when they sin against you, your heavenly Father will also forgive you. But if you do not forgive men their sins, your Father will not forgive your sins"* (Matthew 6:14-15).

This is such a 20th-century problem that I thought the redundancy would be appropriate.

Some first-century disciples undoubtedly would have needed to read and be reminded of this truth regularly. Perhaps none more than those under the direct leadership of the Apostle Paul.

"But he put my sister in jail."

"My dad died—and he ordered it."

"I saw him throw stones at my best friend."

Other Christians were undoubtedly tempted to complain about, then justify their actions in regard to their worldly authorities.

"But the Roman soldiers took my mom and dad when I was 10 and left me alone."

"I could never submit to a government who takes my money and now threatens to take my spouse."

"I refuse to stand for any Roman national anthem."

And God responded to each.

"No forgiveness if you won't forgive."

"No bathing in my love until you shower some forgiveness."

"Stop playing the umpire, and start praying for your Emperor."

First-century prayers ascending to the throne of God seeking forgiveness were rerouted and returned to earth by heavenly messengers if unforgiveness was found in anyone's heart.

Angels still hover nearby, anxious to bring your prayers before the Almighty but with strict orders of non-compromise in this battlefield called forgiveness. You don't. They won't. You do. Then forgiveness.

6) *"Consider therefore the kindness and sternness of God: sternness to those who fell, but kindness to you, provided that you continue in his kindness. Otherwise, you also will be cut off"* (Romans 11:22).

For many, God has become the 98-pound weakling. We think we can pick on him, pounce on him, prey on him and pretty much get away with it. But most of us would not dare use these same tactics with others.

For example, you don't pay your mortgage, they take your house. So you pay the mortgage.

You don't come to work on time, you have got plenty of time now to look for new work. So, you get to work on time.

You don't make your car payment, they take your car.

You skip a practice, you skip a game. You skip another, you skip the season. Skip goes to practice.

We've got more respect for collection agencies, coaches, banks and bosses than we do for God. What we would not dare do to humans, we have done on numerous occasions to God. Millions still adhere to a "once saved always saved" doctrine that permits passive commitment at times, no commitment at others, all with a promise of heaven. If your coach would not swallow that philosophy, why do we think our Creator will?

5) *"For he says to Moses, 'I will have mercy on whom I have mercy and I will have compassion on whom I have compassion'"* (Romans 9:15).

When will the next book be written or sermon preached to explain away this one? Some verses are best left untouched and only feared. Put this is one in the Fear file.

4) *"My conscience is clear, but that does not make me innocent. It is the Lord who judges me"* (1 Corinthians 4:4).

"But my intentions were good."

"I thought I was doing right."

"My heart was good in the matter."

Well, maybe. Maybe not. We are usually not the best judge of our own motives. Certainly we will be pulling for ourselves to be cleared in each situation. And that is exactly why we have the Bible.

One unmarried man's conscience says, "I can go all the way as long as I love her." Another says, "I can do everything but intercourse." Another says, "Just not oral sex." Another says, "It is fine to fondle but only with our clothes on." Another. Another. Another. What do *you* say? *God* says no hint of sexual immorality or impurity of any kind (Ephesians 5:3-4). God says that lust equals adultery (Matthew 5:27-28).

One man's conscience says, "Cheat on your taxes because government cheats on you." Another says, "You don't necessarily need to report it all." Another says, "I will cheat just a little and hope I don't get audited." Another says, "It's just $1,000." Another. Another. God says to submit to governing authorities (Romans 13:1-2), to pay taxes (Romans 13:5-7), and to be above reproach (1 Peter 2:18-22).

One man's conscience says to go to church on Christmas and Easter. Another says, "In the mountains will be fine with just God and me." Another says, "Whenever you can." Another, "Sundays." Another, "Sundays and Wednesdays." Another. Another. Another. God says to take up your cross daily (Luke 9:23-26), give up everything you have (Luke 14:33), encourage one another daily (Hebrews 3:12-13), love him more than all others (Matthew 10:37) and not to stop meeting together (Hebrews 10:23-25).

3) *"God is just: He will pay back trouble to those who trouble you and give relief to you who are troubled...He will punish those who do not know God and do not obey the gospel of our Lord Jesus"* (2 Thessalonians 1:6-8).

Written to all who have thought or are presently thinking they can "get away with it." Paybacks are coming.

To all those who claim ignorance shouting, "I don't know God," God shouts back, "Why not??"

Written to all who feel it unnecessary to obey the gospel or anything under its umbrella. There will be a day of reckoning and accounting for spokesmen of uninvestigated and overly emotional statements akin to some of the following—and more recent "sure things":

"The Titanic will never sink."

"The Hindenburg is indestructible."

"This will be the war to end all wars."

"Man will never walk on the moon."

Just a few of the foolish 20th-century boasts that time humbled. More humbling awaits the boastful owners of loose lips bold enough to take on God.

"God would not let *me* go to hell."

"God does not expect me to be *that* committed."

"I am more morally upright than most."

"God knows if I had the time, I would be more serious."

"God knows that I love her, so sex before marriage is fine."

We had best close our mouths and open our Bibles and get on with knowing and obeying.

2) *"Nothing in all creation is hidden from God's sight. Everything is uncovered and laid bare before the eyes of him to whom we must give account"* (Hebrews 4:13).

The weekend getaways with the boys. God was waiting for you to arrive.

The one-night stand. God watched as you signed the hotel register.

The obscene gesture to your boss behind the closed door. God was sitting on your desk.

The dirty movie at 3:00 a.m. God was not tired.

The fantasizing about your best friend's wife and your neighbor. God monitors your brain.

What could anyone hide from God? Ridiculous thought, isn't it? Yet, surely we all have tried. I hid serious marriage problems for four years while both attending and leading in a church; and in my mind, my reservations for heaven had never been cancelled. I forgot to check with God.

It isn't that difficult to hide things. Not many are looking anyway. Most are too busy hiding their problems and sins as well. But God sees. And God searches. And God stands ready to hear an account. Better get open now before your case is closed.

1) *"In the past God overlooked such ignorance, but now he commands all people everywhere to repent"* (Acts 17:30).

All people. That means *you.*

Everywhere. That's where you sit right now.

Commands. Not suggests, or hopes or wishes.

Repent. That means change, be different. Stop the wrong. Start the right.

God is hard-line all right. But so simple, as well. It really shouldn't be all that confusing. And it isn't. Why, if you have learned to ski, certainly you can learn to repent. If you have graduated, surely you can study your Bible. And if you haven't, go get a fifth-grade reading level and start in. If you can't read, thank God for 20th-century technology, and get the Bible on tape. No tape player? Get a friend and let him read to you.

No excuses. If you can putt a golf ball, you can put some effort into changing. If you have got time to spend at the track, you have also got time to get on track.

God Is Just

10) *"Alexander the metalworker did me a great deal of harm. The Lord will repay him for what he has done"* (2 Timothy 4:14).

God has a sophisticated filing system with names and deeds of his friends and foes. What is in your file? You can know. It is a bit scary, but God will let you know. Open your Bible. Keep reading. You are in there somewhere. You will probably find yourself in a number of places. Galatians 5:19-

21 perhaps? Read it and see. How about Romans 1:29-32 or 2 Timothy 3:1-5?

If you will own up to it, he will own you. If you are willing to change your life, he is willing to change your eternal destiny. But if not, understand that God *will* repay his enemies. His wrath *will* be carried out.

9) *"The Lord will punish men for all such sins, as we have already told you and warned you"* (1 Thessalonians 4:6).

What sins? Just read a little before and after this verse and you'll see. It was sexual sin, and it remains the "biggie" today.

Highschoolers talk about it, pursue it, do it, tell it, then compare experiences with each other.

Members of fraternities and sororities pair up and plan it out.

Single men and women roam the streets, frequent the bars, and take out classified ads, all in hopes of romance and sex.

Married men and women do it with their spouses, then do it with their secretary—or even a stranger.

Men have sex with other men, women with women. Some do both.

Pornography flourishes in a world up to its lustful eyes in sexual sin that will continue to be punished by God.

8) *"Do not be afraid of those who kill the body but cannot kill the soul. Rather, be afraid of the One who can destroy both soul and body in hell"* (Matthew 10:28).

There are certain things I fear.

White-water rafting is one. I've gone three times and thoroughly enjoyed each one. But I feared it—and for good reason. Thousands, over the years, have succumbed to the river's roaring rapids.

I fear heights. Too many have plunged to their deaths for me to climb without caution.

I fear the sun. So I screen it on hot days so my skin will avoid pinkdom, and so I can shower without screaming.

I fear the government so I obey its laws.

I fear failure so I try harder.

I fear death so I look both ways before crossing.

But above all, I must fear God. He made the water. He placed the sun. He sets up the government. He raises the dead. And he holds the keys to both heaven and hell.

7) *"For if God did not spare the natural branches, he will not spare you either"* (Romans 11:21).

Written to any spiritually cocky Gentile who thought God would always be with him regardless of his actions. We all want to be the special cases, don't we?

"Oh, my situation is different."

"Even if others don't, I know I will make it."

"God will give me some extra time to change."

I still have not been to a funeral where the deceased has been proclaimed to have gone to hell. When will someone start telling the truth? If you are not living for God when you die, you do not get to live with him forever. And if you are not living for God today, your past or future religious resume has already been thrown away.

6) *"You adulterous people, don't you know that friendship with the world is hatred toward God? Anyone who chooses to be a friend of the world becomes an enemy of God"* (James 4:4).

I have had my share of enemies. Jim (not his real name) was a big-time bully in high school who constantly picked on me. He outweighed me at least two to one and turned lunch breaks into potential bone breaks. I also faced one in a Cincinnati TV reporter who, from my perspective, was looking to destroy me, my reputation and the people I led by his lies and smear campaigns over a two-year period. Though these and others in my 35 years have brought both worry and wrong, I will welcome these as enemies any day over God.

Just how does God become an enemy? Experiment with the world. Live for money. Forget about heaven. Close your Bible. Make your job top priority. Put family above God.

Start drinking. Take a few drugs. Loosen your stance on purity. Accept all religions as long as they are trying. Do everything God hates, and you have found your enemy.

5) *"For the eyes of the Lord are on the righteous and his ears are attentive to their prayer, but the face of the Lord is against those who do evil"* (1 Peter 3:12).

A staredown. Imagine looking into the eyes of an angry God. Why would God be so ticked and ready to clean our clocks? Simply because we refuse to change, and thus don't challenge others who are doing the same.

Continued, unrepentant evil will lead to many being completely ignored as they pound on the pearly gates on judgment day. You stared God down while alive and still did not change. God has no desire to look into your eyes again.

4) *"Put to death, therefore, whatever belongs to your earthly nature: sexual immorality, impurity, lust, evil desires and greed, which is idolatry. Because of these, the wrath of God is coming"* (Colossians 3:5-6).

The sin of Sodom was punished when the last grain of grace dropped to the bottom of the heavenly hourglass (Genesis 18-19).

The Israelites began 40 years of wandering when they began wondering if God could wipe out their enemies (Numbers 13-14).

The temple of God was destroyed when temple profits superseded temple prophets (Matthew 23-24).

Ananias and Sapphira fell dead when their greed led them on "Mission Impossible" in an effort to pull one over on the Holy Spirit (Acts 5:1-11).

King Herod bathed pridefully in the praise of his constituents and became lunch for the slimy dirt-dwellers (Acts 12:21-23).

Any time sin is not dealt with or put to death, you can guarantee that around some unsuspecting corner, the wrath of God will be revealed and remove the sinner who refuses to remove the sin.

3) *"The wrath of God is being revealed from heaven against all the godlessness and wickedness of men who suppress the truth by their wickedness, since what may be known about God is plain to them, because God has made it plain to them"* (Romans 1:18-19).

Mercy, patience and time for those who may not yet know (though all have or will be given that opportunity); wrath for those who know better. Most of us know better.

We knew it was wrong to have sex before marriage. We just got used to it after all the frequency.

We knew it was wrong to lie. But it helped us temporarily, and usually we didn't get caught. So we continued.

We knew it was wrong to get a divorce. But it was the easy way out and, after all, it was a mutual thing.

We knew it was wrong to slap the kids. But they calmed down and obeyed us when we did it, so we continued.

You knew it was wrong to cheat. You did it because everybody else was. And you made it through school, got a good job, but now you are still cheating. Only this time, it involves your clients.

We have all been guilty of committing the "I know I should not be doing this" sins. But if you are still guilty, my advice is to speed up your repentance, and thus slow down the impending wrath of God.

2) *"For of this you can be sure; no immoral, impure or greedy person—such a man is an idolater, has any inheritance in the kingdom of Christ and of God. Let no one deceive you with empty words, for because of such things God's wrath comes on those who are disobedient"* (Ephesians 5:5-6).

For all those who were not sure, God made sure they could be sure.

The empty-word deceivers. They are still alive today shouting the same stupid statements.

"There really isn't a hell. God is just scaring you into being good just like your parents used to do."

"Hell won't be all that bad."

"You can make it to heaven even if you have sex before marriage."

"You can get drunk occasionally, and God won't care."

"You don't have to give your money to the church. They're probably not using it right anyway."

"Oh, who cares if others think you are greedy or immoral, just as long as *you* know you're not."

"Oh, all teenagers have to go through that stage of rebellion and immorality."

"Oh, a little fun on the side never really hurt anybody, now did it?"

Look out! The angels are unlocking the doors to the lightning storehouses. Missiles of wrath remain available to them on their missions to destroy those who refuse to take God seriously.

1) *"For we know him who said, 'It is mine to avenge. I will repay.' And again, 'The Lord will judge his people. It is a dreadful thing to fall into the hands of the living God"* (Hebrews 10:30-31).

When accidental turns to intentional, the cross turns possible forgiveness into permanent punishment. When a heart has decided to get hard and stay hard, it's hard for God to give out grace. You dare not ask someone for grace who has brutally slaughtered his Son so you can be free to enjoy life here and get a ticket to the hereafter while you slaughter his reputation. Honor God or pay the penalty.

We will all fall into the hands of the living God. Either to be raised and placed in the heavenly realms or lowered to the outer darkness of hell where the wrath of God will remain.

God Is Good

10) *"Command those who are rich in this present world not to be arrogant nor to put their hope in wealth, which is so uncertain, but to put their hope in God, who richly provides us with everything for our enjoyment"* (1 Timothy 6:17).

So much for the "I'll wait till I get to heaven to have a good time" mentality. Who invented the party-pooper God? Who said the Lord can't dance? Who said the lot of a true Christian's life was hum-drum, boring and weird. *Did you?* We have probably all said it at one time or another. But if your understanding of commitment to God is currently at this level, beware of the following interrogation temptations from hell that will be hard to answer—and even harder to overcome.

"Will it be sex or self-control?"

"Will it be money or morality?"

"Will it be booze or the Bible?"

"Are you really enjoying life?"

Who better to look to than God himself for the answers. God knows what you need. He made you, remember? Better yet, he knows the difference between short-term pleasure and lasting joy. After all, who invented the smile? Who created gut-busting laughter? Who put humor into human? Who has more fun than anyone?

Go ahead, I dare you. Leave the alcohol, bury the plans of seeing how far you can get on your next date, turn down the drug offer, and keep the sin-money in your billfold. Find a Bible, learn about God and surround yourself with others who have learned the secret of real fun. Watch out, you might just have a good time.

9) *"Now it is God who has made us for this very purpose and has given us the Spirit as a deposit, guaranteeing what is to come"* (2 Corinthians 5:5).

A repeat from Chapter Four. Haven't forgot it already, have you?

Here it is again, just in case the frown has found its way back to your face. Satan cringes when people read this verse. He loses when people understand it. God made you to go to heaven. He has got greatness and eternity clearly marked on your map.

At the moment of any conception, another name is added

to the inheritance document. God wants everybody in. He will fight to keep you on the list. He has hired a great, "never lost a case before" lawyer in Jesus. His angels are the perfect private eyes. Perceived circumstances are calculated strategies of heaven to keep you in the will. Earthly failures are heaven's way of helping you succeed eternally. You have no clue what God has done to help you make it to heaven. Sherlock Holmes could offer no answer as to what God is up to. Colombo would be confused. And even more, you have no idea what God will do from this moment forward to make sure you arrive safely.

8) *"I now realize how true it is that God does not show favoritism, but accepts men from every nation who fear him and do what is right"* (Acts 10:34-35).

Cornelius must have turned cartwheels upon hearing this. "I can go, too? I can go, too! We all can go! Yippee!!"

The Gentiles were in. They could go to heaven. Of course they could! Somebody just forgot to tell Peter and the rest of the Jews. So God did. One typical afternoon on a rooftop God met Peter and put an end to prejudice and the rumors of a narrow-minded God. Now, if the kingdom key-holder was off-centered on his views about God, you can see how susceptible the rest of us are.

Red. Yellow. Black. White.

Good guys. Bad guys. Black hats. White hats.

Religious. Non-religious. Semi-religious.

Rich. Poor.

Young. Old.

Inner city. Suburbanites.

Employed. Unemployed.

Smart. Dumb.

White collar. Blue collar. No collar.

Athletes. Nerds. Cheerleaders. Trombone players.

Pulitzer Prize winners. Door-prize winners.

Super Bowl victors. Popcorn and peanut vendors.

Pilots. Airport security guards.

Policemen. Prisoners.

CEOs. Tellers.

Magna Cum Laude graduates. "I barely made it" graduates.

Ministers. New converts.

Hollywooders. Homeless.

Presidents. PTA members.

Construction corporate chiefs. Ditch diggers.

Highway architects. Flagmen.

Oh, there is plenty of room for all kinds.   Give God a prejudice X-ray and it would turn up negative.

7) *"...God does not judge by external appearance..."* (Galatians 2:6).

Now, wouldn't that be unfair? If God based salvation on sex-appeal, the only women in heaven would be those types on beer commercials and billboards. Only those who had the time and money for the three to five times a week at the local health club would pass heaven's final inspection. The rest of us would suck it in some places and flex it in others, only to discover the final test on judgment day would be taken while breathing out.

Thank God looks are not everything. Maybe more appropriately, looks are nothing.

Big nose? Big deal. God does not take time to measure it, even if you do.

Receding hairline? Get a transplant or hairpiece if you want, God still numbers only your real ones.

Too short? Zacchaeus made it.

Too tall? Just don't act like Goliath, and you should be okay.

Hips too wide? Hair too coarse? Too light? Too dark? Scars? Pimples? Wearing only hand-me-downs? Only able to buy used everything?

In a world where all the above have topped the scales in significance, it's great to be under the authority of the One who really only cares about the heart.

6) *"For everything God created is good, and nothing is to be rejected if it is received with thanksgiving"* (1 Timothy 4:4).

It would be impossible for anything else to be true. If God is inherently good, it would become impossible for anything he created to be bad.

"Well, what about garbage dumps?"

Don't dump your garbage on God.

"What about people? What happened? Why all the murders and violence?"

How many cold-blooded killings have been committed by pre-schoolers?

"Molestations? Look at all the abuse."

How many kindergartners have abused their parents?

"Poverty? There are so many poor people."

How many elementary schoolers throw away their lives and gamble away their paychecks?

Isn't it interesting that when God does good, man seeks to take the credit, and when man does bad, he gives God the blame. Everything started off good. Every human started off good. But after years of Satan and seduction, only one good remains—God.

5) *"God is not unjust; he will not forget your work and the love you have shown him as you have helped his people and continue to help them"* (Hebrews 6:10).

My favorite people are the ones who notice me and remember me. A little selfish, I know, but I am pretty sure you are not far behind. The ones who don't forget to say Thanks. The ones who send the cards thanking you for that special "something" you did 10 years ago. They still remember!

Been forgotten lately? You are probably not alone.

The wives who raise the kids and keep the household together but receive little help and no praise from their husbands.

The child promised a reward for a good report card still waiting weeks later.

The employee vowed a raise in five months if progressing satisfactorily. It is now a new time frame and a new definition of satisfactory.

The friend waiting for a response from another, this now his sixth letter.

The single woman destined to be the ideal spouse who has not been asked out in months.

The son promised a game of catch, but Dad had to catch another plane.

God never forgets. You ask. He answers. You seek. He supplies. You knock. He knocks down the obstacle. While others may have checked you off their list, or allowed you or your deed to be erased from memory, God has all your efforts stored neatly in his colossal computer. You are not forgotten by a good God.

4) *"...God our Father, who loved us and by his grace gave us eternal encouragement and good hope..."* (2 Thessalonians 2:16).

Everybody needs encouragement, but sadly, few receive it. How many people have an "inspiration" in their lives? Someone who will not quit on them when they quit on themselves.

How many divorces could have been cancelled if an encourager were nearby?

How many suicide bullets and bottles could have been thrown away if a hopeful phone number could have been dialed?

How many architects' blueprints for juvenile delinquent centers could have been burned if parents had decided to encourage and not exasperate?

How much money could have been saved on prison expansion if just one encourager were there to point a potential inmate in a positive direction?

But one has always been there—God. If Mom and Dad are not clapping, the angels' cymbals are. If your spouse has not sent you a card, God wrote you a Bible to tell you what he thinks of you. If your child ignores you, remember God's child died for you. If your coach only criticizes, God attends every game and fills the stadium with energetic angels. And when heaven hollers, it's plenty loud to hear. Stop pouting, and start listening.

3) *"This is love for God: to obey his commands. And his commands are not burdensome"* (1 John 5:3).

I wonder how many of us really believe that being a hard-line follower of God and obedient to the Bible is a burden. The "I'm in God's box and don't have room to breathe" syndrome. Now, either this verse is true, or it isn't. To obey the Bible is freeing. It is not *too* difficult. It is not an impossibility. It is not *too* tough. It is not taxing.

What's more of a burden, anyway?

Saying No to the temptation of drunkenness, or waking up with a hangover?

Keeping your hormones in check, or having the doctor confirm what the home test already revealed?

Turning the other cheek, or checking into jail?

Telling the truth, or covering your tracks?

Investing your money in spiritual endeavors, or sweating over today's stock market report?

Being totally committed to a church and all its activities, or figuring out what you can do with all your time?

Disciplining your kids, or staying up late hoping and praying that they didn't do anything "too stupid"?

Inviting someone to come to church, or feeling guilty for passing up another opportunity?

The burden actually lies in *not obeying* rather than obeying. God planned it that way. So the next time you're hung-up on how there are just too many commandments, read 1 John 5:3 again and hang up on Satan.

2) *"If you, then, though you are evil, know how to give good gifts to your children, how much more will your Father in heaven give good gifts to those who ask him!"* (Matthew 7:11).

Most of us are "spoilers." So is God. He loves to spoil us. Not to our downfall, of course, but spoiling is his nature. Unfortunately, most of us have so convinced ourselves that

God will never spoil us, we forgot to believe that God loves to give, and sadly we give more "giving" credit to evil parents.

How many of us overspend for our kids during Christmas? How many say Yes to a toy after 100 Nos? It's our job to give gifts. To pile on the love. To spoil a little. Who, then, made God out to be any different? Certainly this verse can set the record straight. God is good and has gifts to prove it.

1) *"No temptation has seized you except what is common to man. And God is faithful; he will not let you be tempted beyond what you can bear. But when you are tempted, he will also provide a way out so that you can stand up under it"* (1 Corinthians 10:13).

My favorite verse in all the Bible. It sets me up and sets me straight on a regular basis. It eliminates excuses. Never again can I say, "It's too tough." No more pieces of straw for the camel's back. No more, "I can't say No to this" or "I'm too weak right now to overcome." This verse will change your life if you let it. Complaining will fade away. Negativity will be nuked. Answers will be sought out. Plans will be derived. Hope will return. Success will be found.

"I have to commit adultery."

Why?

"I can't stop drinking."

Who told you that?

"It's impossible to forgive my parents."

Who gave birth to that idea?

"I will always struggle with lust, impurity and sexual immorality."

Who started that scandal?

"I have to fly off the handle!!"

No, you need to get a handle.

Excuses and blameshifting are for non-believers. Those who love *blaming* more than *believing*. You can say No. A good God will give you all the help you need.

The New. My prayer is that these verses will bring you a new perspective. God's dream is that they will bring you a new life.

Chapter Nine

The Psalms

"Lift up your heads, O you gates; be lifted up,
you ancient doors, that the King of glory may come in.
Who is this King of glory? The LORD strong and
mighty, the LORD mighty in battle. Lift up your heads,
O you gates, lift them up, you ancient doors, that the
King of glory may come in. Who is he, this King of
glory? The LORD Almighty—he is the King of glory"
(Psalm 24:7-10).

The Psalms.

From the deep, dark recesses of a cave to the comforts of a castle, 150 gems of the heart written for choirs and concert presentations.

A collection of man's ups and downs, highs and lows, fears and follies, mistakes and marvels.

Pleas for persecutors to be crushed and pain to subside.

Requests for new hearts, new songs and new beginnings.

A masterpiece of man's most precious and painful moments.

Written while searching for God and searching for answers.

David at his best and David at his worst. David on God. David on creation. David in prayer. David on repentance. David on the Bible.

Moses, the sons of Korah, and a few others make cameo appearances, but mainly one man reveals his relationship to a mighty God. It is real. It is powerful. And it is bound to change your life. Whether at this moment you are cave-dwelling or cake-walking, the book of Psalms will touch your heart and further introduce you to an incredible God.

God Is Holy

10) *"Great is the LORD and most worthy of praise; his greatness no one can fathom"* (Psalm 145:3).

Once you have dug deep in the word of God, seen, heard and experienced his love and understood his phenomenal power, keep going. God and his greatness have no ocean floor. The bottomless sea of love.

9) *"How awesome is the LORD Most High, the great King over all the earth"* (Psalm 47:2).

The surfer's description of a killer wave.

The giggly sophomore's analysis of a recent date with the senior quarterback.

The fanatic crowd's reference to a Michael Jordan dunk.

Awesome. Awesome. Awesome.

Overused. Overused. Overused.

I use it too. But "awesome" needs to be reserved for God and his works. After all, who gave Mr. All-American his looks and charm? Who knit Michael Jordan together in his mother's womb? Who made the killer wave? Deity, dude.

8) *"And the words of the LORD are flawless, like silver refined in a furnace of clay, purified seven times"* (Psalm 12:6).

No cat ever got his tongue. No feline found a flaw and never will. Never a "Oh, let me rephrase that please." No statement retractions. No practice speeches. His words are eloquent, efficient, effective, and eternal.

You and I search for the words and fumble them when we find them. We have outlines, rough drafts, rewrites and final copies. Still imperfect. God has perfect sentence structure, perfect analogies, perfect phraseology. Perfect. Perfect. Perfect.

7) *"Praise be to the LORD God, the God of Israel, who alone does marvelous deeds"* (Psalm 72:18).

Sounds like we might need to change our vocabularies. First "awesome," now "marvelous." Let's all at once, now, move ourselves out of that "marvelous deed doers" category. Feel a shift in the earth's core?

Great? Perhaps. Marvelous? Only one is capable.

Took a cup of water to a thirsty soul? Good job. Good deed.

Parted the Red Sea? Marvelous.

Visited someone sick in the hospital? Good for you.

Raised the dead after four days of death? Marvelous.

Helped to tear down an abandoned building in the name of progress and renewal? Great job.

Collapsed the walls of Jericho with no dynamite? Marvelous.

6) *"You are resplendent with light, more majestic than mountains rich with game"* (Psalm 76:4).

Now there is one you may need Webster's help with. "Resplendent." Go ahead and look it up. After you get it, you still won't get it.

Most of us have probably never described ourselves that way simply because we either didn't know the word or couldn't pronounce it. Whatever it really means, one thing is for sure— it must be a whole lot of light. Lamp factory workers, light bulb manufacturers, electricity know-it-alls, sun studiers and stargazers combined could not contemplate the quantities of light in our Holy God.

Go ahead and turn them on, all at once. Every last light in the world. Still only a weak-battery flashlight in comparison to the light of a resplendent God.

5) *"For a thousand years in your sight are like a day that has just gone by, or like a watch in the night"* (Psalm 90:4).

So, if man has been here 10,000 years (very debatable, I know, but someone else can write a book about that) that makes God 10. Ten *days* old, that is! While all the greats of history come and go, God is just getting started. That may explain how God has had the patience and energy to keep humbling all of those prideful world leaders of the past.

When Egypt's Pharaoh took him on, God was one or two. A few minutes later he removed every arrogant king from Promised Land territory so his people could move in. Shortly thereafter, God rocked the world with a killer rock in Goliath's forehead. He celebrated his third birthday with Nebuchadnezzar's downfall, and a little later, left a finger-painted message of doom for Babylon's Belshazzar. Moments later the great I AM plotted strategies against Alexander the Great. And only minutes ago, he brought about the fall of Hitler and his Third Reich.

4) *"From heaven the LORD looks down and sees all mankind; from his dwelling place he watches all who live on the earth—he who forms the hearts of all, who considers everything they do"* (Psalm 33:13-15).

The shot from the Goodyear Blimp with a telephoto lens, developed, blown up and analyzed. A bird's-eye view with an eagle eye. On the stadium's top row with biggie binoculars, assessing this game called Life.

What does God see when you are up to bat?

3) *"For you are great and do marvelous deeds; you alone are God"* (Psalm 86:10).

Though many have aggressively run for the office, the position has never been vacant. One God never elected but in nonetheless.

No votes. No campaigns. No commercials. No conventions. God is Mr. President and he cannot be impeached. He can never be dismissed. He will not be voted out. No two-term limitations. God is not only the president, he is also the ultimate Supreme Court judge in for the duration—eternity.

So put your signs down, rip up your flowery speeches, and stop the campaign rhetoric. You are free to do what you want, but you are not free to vote for the universal presidency or against his policies.

2) *"Our God is in heaven; he does whatever pleases him"* (Psalm 115:3).

We all are very familiar with our "superiors."

So you want to go 90? Then get ready to pay $250.

Feel like extending your vacation? Get ready for a permanent one.

If God wants to forgive, it is done. If God wants to humble, it, too, is done. Should God want to destroy, done again. If God wants to save, done. If God wants to bless, done. If God wants to curse, done.

No bosses. No accountability. No report card. No evaluation.

1) *"Who is like the LORD our God, the One who sits enthroned on high, who stoops down to look on the heavens and the earth?"* (Psalm 113:5-6).

Just how big is God?

Bigger than a bulldozer, but not looking to clear you out.

Bigger than any mountain, but he won't make you climb up to find him.

Bigger than all the oceans, but not buried at the bottom of the sea.

Bigger than the moon, but accessible to more than a few.

Bigger than the earth, but not spinning in a circle.

Bigger than the sun, but no desire to burn you.

Bigger than the Milky Way, yet moments from your heart.

God Is Powerful

10) *"Praise him for his acts of power; praise him for his surpassing greatness"* (Psalm 150:2).

How much power did it take to make the sun? What had to occur for dust to become Doug? Who can make a Rita from a rib? Who can talk to water and make it divide? Who can make the sun stand still and humans still stand it? Who can float tasty wafers from his heavenly bakery to starving desert nomads? Who can bring water from a rock by stick or by shout? Who can turn tears to triumph at a crowded fu-

neral? Who can wake up the coffin-dwellers? Who can walk
on water, make wine from water, calm the water, and save by
water? Only the Maker of water.

9) *"Great is our LORD and mighty in power; his understanding
has no limit"* (Psalm 147:5)
    Just how smart is God?
    Could there be a heart problem God could not cure?
Heart specialists today perform countless life-saving opera-
tions around the clock. They understand the heart and how it
ticks. Yet God monitors *theirs* while they repair others. I wonder, then, how effective would God be operating as a surgeon?
    What broken relationship could God not glue? What
world issue or concern could God not fix? Famine? Wars?
Prejudice? How do you feed the kids? How do you silence
the guns? How do you color coordinate a multi-colored
world? How do you stay happy? How do you *get* happy?
    All the answers to the above questions are found in the
Bible. The problem lies, then, not in the limit of his understanding, but instead, in the limit of our acceptance.

8) *"The LORD is my light and my salvation—whom shall I fear?
The LORD is the stronghold of my life—of whom shall I be afraid?"*
(Psalm 27:1).
    We fear so much. People, places, things. We fear nouns.
Crazy, isn't it?
    The boss, Mom, Dad, the neighbor.
    The alley, the ghetto, the prison.
    School, death, report cards, failure, water, fat, change,
future, loneliness, pain—and the list goes on.
    If I missed yours, go ahead and write it in. You fear
something. But with unlimited access to a God of power who
opts to be unselfish with it, the ultimate in protection can
become a reality and confidence can become your partner.

7) *"Through you we push back our enemies; through your name
we trample our foes"* (Psalm 44:5).

How many stories do we have to read (and how many times?) about how God's people gained victories with even the silliest of battle plans until we realize that God needs no guns, bazookas or Star Wars laser technology to overcome the enemy?

Consider this possible "around the campfire chat" the day before one of Israel's biggest battles against the Amalekites (Exodus 17:8-15):

"Okay, who are our best men?

"Moses, Aaron and Hur are, of course, God."

"Alright, you three guys stay back. Moses, you sit down, and raise up your arms. Aaron and Hur, you keep vigilant watch and when Mo loses momentum, lift those tired arms back up (plug your nose if you need to) until I tell you to stop."

Put that one in the win column.

God was again up to his old tricks just a few years later in Israel vs. Jericho (Judges 7-8).

"Do we have the seven trumpets? Have you all been practicing your shouting? Let's hear it one more time...Okay, great! Now here is the itinerary, guys. Monday, we march around Jericho. All of us."

"Hey, Josh, can we take our weapons, please?"

"Yeah, sure, but you won't need to use them."

"Now for today, Tuesday—same thing." "Wednesday—ditto—continue marching." "Thursday—I know this sounds crazy, men, but we are going to do it again."

"Murmur, murmur, rumble, rumble."

"Friday—keep those boots shined because we are going for another stroll around the city."

"Saturday—the weekend. Walk!"

"Sunday—guys, you are going to love this. We are going to do overtime today, men. 'Seven laps,' says the Lord. Trumpet players—I want you saving up your breath because you will be blowing for a real, long time. After lap seven, one long trumpet blast. Make it good. Al Hirt and Chuck Mangione will have nothing on you guys. Okay, now here is the good part. When they get done, everybody else will begin shouting as loud as they can. You know, just like your Mom and Dad did when they were at that huge party Aaron had while Moses was mountain climbing."

"Yeah. Well. With all due respect, then what, sir?"

"Nothing."

"Nothing, sir?"

"Nothing. That's all God said. Well, except that we would win."

And win they did, as the Jericho wall crashed and crumbled and with it the city's short-lived dynasty.

Gideon, with just 300 of an available 30,000 men, using torches, trumpets and the sound of broken glass, destroyed an entire army.

You don't need a gun, you need a God. You don't need a knife, just some knowledge. Not bombs, but brains. Brains to figure out God's got enough power for you to be a winner every time.

6) *"Say to God, 'How awesome are you deeds! So great is your power that your enemies cringe before you'"* (Psalm 66:3).

During my junior year of high school, I had the opportunity to play on the varsity basketball team. I was not quite good enough to crack the starting five but still found plenty of playing time. We had a good team that year and finished the regular season with a record of 18-2. Most of our opponents knew that when they came to our gymnasium, they would ride their bus back in defeat. A 50-game home court winning streak stared them in the face, combined with the more obvious fact—we had much better players.

But it was especially true when Rainier, Washington, came one evening for a nice, friendly game of round ball. We had already defeated them on their home court by 30 points earlier in the year, so our confidence was at an all-time high. At the end of the first quarter it was 25-2. Their players were looking for opportunities to find bench time. Time-outs were treasured.

At the half, we led 37-4. We got chewed out for giving up four. The truth is, it could have been 37-0, but we got lazy a couple times on defense. Due to the ongoing slaughter, I got plenty of playing time and when time expired the scoreboard showed 78-9. We held them under double figures. Never had that been done before in the recent history of our league. It may never be done again. We knew we would win, but not quite with that type of complete domination.

Sounds a lot like a game between God and any who try to join his league. So, the next time you think you might be in trouble, or you have decided to give up in your heart, or you sin so much that your diseased heart creates a wimpy, non-powerful God who cannot pop you out of your present pickle, remember one word—Rainier. Then go get God and get on with your victory. Send Satan and his demons back whining on their bus to hell.

5) *"I was pushed back and about to fall, but the LORD helped me. The LORD is my strength and my song; he has become my salvation"* (Psalm 118:13-14).

When life's thugs are beating on your door, hang on to this one.

When the troublemaker named Divorce has made you feel worthless and pushed you to private pain, God is very near.

When the gang called Financial Doom surrounds you and laughs at you all the way to the bank, look around, God must be very near.

When the demons of Quit, Cancel and Complain hold out the surrender papers for you to sign, look for the angel of truth at your side, eager to share with you news of a powerful God who has plenty available to help you overcome any adversity known to man.

4) *"God is our refuge and strength, an ever-present help in trouble"* (Psalm 46:1).

Trouble! And who does not have some? Most of us have plenty. Trouble at home. At work. At play.

In the car. With the car.
Trying to get a vacation. On vacation.
Having to move. The move. After the move.
Having kids. Raising kids.
Getting friends. Keeping friends.
Finding a spouse. Loving a spouse.
Trouble is everywhere. But then again, according to this verse, so is God.

3) *"Praise be to the LORD my Rock, who trains my hands for war, my fingers for battle. He is my loving God and my fortress, my stronghold and my deliverer, my shield, in whom I take refuge, who subdues peoples under me"* (Psalm 144:1-2).

Even your fingers are important to God. Down to the little pinky, he gives us what we need to fight the battles.

2) *"With your help I can advance against a troop; with my God I can scale a wall"* (Psalm 18:29).

The Berlin Walls of the spiritual world still stand for billions of misguided souls. The wall between freedom and bondage that many have decided to stop scaling. You tried hard once but got shot down. And though you don't really like where you're at right now, you've grown afraid and somewhat accustomed to it. Go buy another rope, get a new spirit, and get back to climbing.

Maybe it's a drug wall. Go get some more help.

Or, perhaps, a commitment wall. Go after it again with renewed zeal.

A relationship wall? Pick up the phone, and do your part to make amends.

A doctrinal wall? Read the passage again, and just do what it says.

A leadership wall? Go ask someone for a new responsibility, and get back in the battle.

1) *"One thing God has spoken, two things I have heard: that you, O God, are strong, and that you, O LORD, are loving"* (Psalm 62:11-12).

You have heard it for the 30th time now. Isn't it time to believe? God is powerful.

God Is Caring

10) *"Praise be to the LORD, to God our Savior, who daily bears our burdens"* (Psalm 68:19).

This verse is very good news for many reasons:

1. We have burdens.
2. We have lots of burdens.
3. We have burdens every day.
4. We have lots of burdens every day.
5. We cannot handle our burdens by ourselves.

We need someone to bear them when life becomes a bear.

If God used the phone, you would talk, or at least get a message on your recorder every day. If God sent mail, your steps would find bounce once again heading to the mailbox. Messages left and letters sent from the Lord, complete with instructions on how to relax and plans on how to persevere.

9) *"For this God is our God for ever and ever; he will be our guide even to the end"* (Psalm 48:14).

When will God quit trying? Only at your funeral when your tear ducts are closed and others' are opened. Then he will quickly turn his attention to the living.

Sadly, too many quit on God just prior to the prize because they believe God has quit on them. Read it one more time.

If you're a sports fan, you can never justify quitting or giving up. Too much video proof of "Hail Mary" passes completed (what would she think of this term?) and last-ditch efforts succeeded. Too many 30-point comebacks. Too many fourth place teams in mid-season that eventually became World Champions.

Abraham Lincoln suffered five political defeats, two mental breakdowns, numerous family deaths and other major setbacks before being elected President in 1860. One man's perseverance proves to us all that it *can* be done and points us back to our Guide.

Be like Abe. Honest, it works. You don't quit—God won't either.

8) *"The LORD is close to the brokenhearted and saves those who are crushed in spirit"* (Psalm 34:18).

Broken hearts. Broken dreams.

The baby you had many dreams for has Downs.

Grandpa died, and fishing just isn't the same anymore.

The abortion that seemed so right, now haunts you.

You see another spot on the mammogram. You've seen it before, but you beat it. Can you do it again?

Another person you loved and brought to the Lord has now left him and left you.

Another relationship you had such high hopes for will not end in marriage.

Spirit-crushing moments that make it impossible to smile, clap, leap or hope. God has his Daytimer full of appointments with people just like you.

7) *"The LORD is a refuge for the oppressed, a stronghold in times of trouble. Those who know your name will trust in you, for you, LORD, have never forsaken those who seek you"* (Psalm 9:9-10).

You will need a stronghold when a weak link is exposed in your chain. How is your chain these days? Did some unexpected event damage your chain? Keep seeking because the promise remains intact. You seek. He cares. You trust. He repairs. Soon your chain will be as good as new.

6) *"You hear, O LORD, the desire of the afflicted; you encourage them, and you listen to their cry, defending the fatherless and the oppressed, in order that man, who is of the earth, may terrify no more"* (Psalm 10:17-18).

Life without Dad can be scary. I have never been there, but know many who have. The younger you are, the more challenging it is, but Dad dying and leaving a child fatherless at any age can prove to be traumatic. Two of my best friends are there.

Jeff's dad died four years ago. He put a gun to his head two days before he was to be married a second time. A successful man with lots of money but who was hurting and decided to escape from his private pain. His wife had died of cancer three years earlier. Jeff now had no Mom or Dad, so I adopted him. Why? Because I believe this verse. No, there are no signed papers or official documents, only solemn vows that I promise to act and provide for him exactly as his earthly father would.

Aaron's dad died about a year ago. He had a massive heart attack while doing business in a New Jersey bank. Routine questions like, "Where do your parents live?" and "What are you doing for the holidays?" are now reminders to him of what is not there anymore. I adopted Aaron, too. Everybody needs a dad.

If you happen to be feeling fatherless, hang on to this verse and know that God is working to take your fears, loneliness and insecurities and replace them with encouraging thoughts and direction for the remaining days of your life. Congratulations! You can be adopted.

5) *"He reached down from on high and took hold of me; he drew me out of deep waters. He rescued me from my powerful enemy, from my foes, who were too strong for me. They confronted me in the day of my disaster. But the LORD was my support. He brought me into a spacious place; he rescued me because he delighted in me"* (Psalm 18:16-19).

God, the rescuer. Not a mouse looking for a little girl in a Disney movie, but a mighty God looking for adults in a dying world.

Houses on fire with abuse and adultery, and a God going in to look for the heart who hurts.

Dormitories on fire with immorality, worldliness and exclusion, and a God going in to find the coed who cares.

High schools on fire with peer pressure, ostracizing and sexual sin, and a God going in to find the future church leader looking for a change.

4) *"Cast your cares on the* LORD *and he will sustain you; he will never let the righteous fall"* (Psalm 55:22).

We all need regular sustaining. You probably got some and did not even realize it.

A move to another city just before depression.

A raise only days before you would be tempted to cut your contribution.

A good date just before you decided to harden your heart to marriage.

A three-day cottage getaway just before the devil's plan to lead you on a permanent church getaway.

God knows what we need and when we need it. And he cares enough to do something about it.

3) *"Record my lament; list my tears on your scroll—are they not in your record?"* (Psalm 56:8).

The bucket brigade. Angels assigned to comfort humans with heavy hearts and catch their tears. They carry buckets. Back and forth. Every tear ever cried is caught, weighed and recorded. Heaven's happiest angels, gladly obeying marching orders to visit the homes of the hurting.

2) *"You give me your shield of victory, and your right hand sustains me; you stoop down to make me great. You broaden the path beneath me so that my ankles do not turn"* (Psalm 18:35-36).

So good it makes our list twice. Suffered any sprains since Chapter Seven? Probably. So here is some more tape!

A God who will take the time, not just to make us great, but show us how to be great.

A God who could have shouted it from the heavens but descended instead in human form.

A God who could have taught sacrifice but instead showed us how to endure suffering.

A God who uses no megaphones, VCRs, or multi-media presentations. He touches, then teaches. Then he takes your hand and shows you how.

1) *"A father to the fatherless, a defender of widows, is God in his holy dwelling. God sets the lonely in families, he leads forth the prisoners with singing"* (Psalm 68:5-6).

The orphan, the widow, the lonely, and the locked-up—God spends much of his time with the people we typically ignore.

Do you believe it by now? You have had 30 chances. But because of all we have just read, my guess is that he will give you even more.

God Is Hard Line

10) *"The LORD has chastened me severely, but he has not given me over to death"* (Psalm 118:18).

This nearly made the "Caring" top 10. He chastens because he wants you to change. He is hoping for better, but he must discipline to get you there. He did it to David, a "man after his own heart." An earthly king of kings under the leadership of the eternal King of kings was humbled through suffering. The one who slew the giant and guided God's people to greatness had to be severely chastened.

God does spank. From time to time we are going to need to just drop our drawers, grab our ankles, and hang on. We may need a lot of swats to save our spots in heaven.

9) *"They angered him with their high places; they aroused his jealousy with their idols. When God heard them, he was very angry; he rejected Israel completely"* (Psalm 78:58-59).

Rejected. Turned away. Refused entrance. The Israelites had a ticket to the show but brought along some idols as well. God hates idols. He turns away heaven's ticket-holders of today with idols packed away in their bags.

God is the gate-watcher. If you plan on coming to the game with your idols, plan on being asked to leave. And, unlike many ushers at sporting events, God will make you undergo a thorough search for any unacceptable stadium paraphernalia. He looks for the idols of jealousy.

First God's questions. Then his scrutiny.

"Got any job idols in there?"

"I know you go to church, but what is in your bag?"

"Let me check that Daytimer. Overtime. Appointments. Vacation."

"Where is prayer?"

"Where is studying the Bible every day."

"Where is time with me in the middle of the week?"

"Got any money idols in there?"

"I know you give every Sunday, but what is in your bag?"

"Oh, your IRA bank book."

"You have $50,000 in there but have no plans to give any of that?"

"Let me see your car payment booklet."

"So, now we see the real reason you lowered your contribution the last five years."

"Any family idols in there?"

"I know you bring your family to church—just open your bag."

"Is this the schedule for your son's practices? And you are the coach, right?"

"Lucy's piano recital is coming up soon, isn't it? You always wanted to play when you were a kid, didn't you?"

"And you are a PTA board member."

"So when did you have your last family devotional?"

"How often do you discipline your kids?"

"When was the last time you prayed with them?"

"What kind of example are you setting for them?"

The evidence is often overwhelming. Undeniable proof of the many gods that arouse the one God to jealousy.

8) *"The LORD is known by his justice; the wicked are ensnared by the work of their hands"* (Psalm 9:16).

God's reputation is riding on his justice. On his hard-line stand on truth, purity, commitment and change. Don't plan on him ruining his reputation.

7) *"You are not a God who takes pleasure in evil; with you the*

wicked cannot dwell" (Psalm 5:4-5).

While humans laugh off drunkenness, heaven's hatred for it intensifies.

While young men brag about how many they have slept with, God brings your judgment book to his desk.

While you breathe a sigh of relief for not being caught by your boss or caught by your wife, the Lord breathes fire and vengeance.

God is not happy with any sin or sinner. If they won't look to change, he will look to destroy.

6) *"He observes the sons of men; his eyes examine them. The LORD examines the righteous, but the wicked and those who love violence his soul hates"* (Psalm 11:4-5).

It should be crystal clear by now—you don't mess with God.

He hates. He punishes. He examines. Many say it is an impossibility to be hated by God. Read it again.

5) *"From heaven the LORD looks down and sees all mankind; from his dwelling place he watches all who live on the earth—he who forms the hearts of all, who considers everything they do"* (Psalm 33:13-15).

Angels assigned to your life with video camera, a long playing tape, and the works. Top quality. Latest design. The red light never goes off. Daily delivered to the banquet room where huge screen televisions (somewhere around five billion) play simultaneously.

What did God see today? Yesterday? (Thank God the video cameras also work when we are doing right!)

Change today, if necessary. Let God enjoy his viewing.

4) *"You rebuke and discipline men for their sin; you consume their wealth like a moth—each man is but a breath"* (Psalm 39:11).

Nobody will get away with murder or any other of the "lesser" sins. God's nature says that if you sin, you will get disciplined. Unlike most parents, sentimentality is not part of God's character. If you need a rebuke, you *will* hear from God. If you need some discipline, you *will* visit his office.

3) *"O LORD our God, you answered them; you were to Israel a forgiving God, though you punished their misdeeds"* (Psalm 99:8).

Imagine where our world would be today if God were not in the punishing business. Imagine where you would be. Though nobody ever claimed to like it, we all need it. I wonder if God says, "This is going to hurt me a lot more than it is going to hurt you"? Sounds consistent doesn't it? Only when he says it, he really means it.

2) *"To the faithful you show yourself faithful, to the blameless you show yourself blameless, to the pure you show yourself pure, but to the crooked you show yourself shrewd. You save the humble but bring low those whose eyes are haughty"* (Psalm 18:25-27).

Door #1—The Faithful God.

Door #2—The Blameless God.

Door #3—The Pure God.

Which door will it be? All are great choices. No "clunkers" today! Unfortunately, many looking to be contestants will not be welcome in God's studio.

Only the faithful get in. Those always willing to get up no matter how hard the fall.

The blameless can come, too. Those striving for perfection and hating it horribly when they miss.

And finally, the pure. Those open with all their trash and completely unable to be blackmailed.

1) *"But from everlasting to everlasting the LORD's love is with those who fear him, and his righteousness with their children's children—with those who keep his covenant and remember to obey his precepts"* (Psalm 103:17-18).

There are conditions.

"Fear him" —having a tremendous undying respect for the One who holds the keys to heaven and hell and ultimately decides which will be your destination.

"Keep his covenant" —you made a deal, now live up to it.

"Remember to obey" —forgetting is not an excuse.

God Is Just

10) *"God's anger rose against them; he put to death the sturdiest among them, cutting down the young men of Israel"* (Psalm 78:31).

I have to believe that many coroner's reports today are only partially correct. What was the *actual* cause of death? The reports and the obituaries may disagree, but my Bible says that God puts to death as well. What is accidental and unfortunate to man may be intentional and just in the eyes of God.

9) *"But God will shoot them with arrows; suddenly they will be struck down"* (Psalm 64:7-8).

The Righteous Robin Hood of retribution. Bull's-eye. Just make sure you're not robbing from the poor and giving to the rich. You could become target practice for the archer of the archenemy.

8) *"You destroy those who tell lies; bloodthirsty and deceitful men the LORD abhors"* (Psalm 5:6).

Liars will lie to themselves, claiming this verse cannot be true.

Bloodthirsty men will make no time to check it out as they plan for their next conquest.

Deceitful men will convince themselves that this verse does not apply to them.

All three are bound for destruction.

7) *"Who knows the power of your anger? For your wrath is as great as the fear that is due you"* (Psalm 90:11).

So everybody is going to heaven, are they? So God probably will change his mind on judgment day and be loving and not wrathful. So even some in hell right now might be able to get to heaven eventually?

Who invented the lies? That question is easy. Who believes them? Only you can answer that.

6) *"The wicked plot against the righteous and gnash their teeth at them; but the LORD laughs at the wicked, for he knows their day* *is coming"* (Psalm 37:12-13).

Certainly God must chuckle (and at times cry) when we quote the ever-popular "He who laughs last, laughs best."

Pharaoh laughed at Moses' request to take the two million slaves for a weekend retreat in the mountains. God laughed at his chariot's baptism.

Jezebel laughed at Elijah's message from the Lord. God laughed as the Dobermans drank her blood.

Nebuchadnezzar laughed in the lap of luxury, mocking the Lord and drinking from sacred goblets. God laughed as he watched the once-great king graze with the cows.

People still laugh today. They laugh at a Christian's radical commitment. They laugh at the upside-down teachings of sacrifice and self-denial. They laugh as they encounter women serious about God and serious about their virginity, then mock their "missing out" status.

But God laughs the loudest. Join him and laugh off the persecution and cutting remarks. Then get ready for one hilarious eternity.

5) *"God, who is enthroned forever, will hear them and afflict them—men who never change their ways and have no fear of God"* (Psalm 55:19).

Who will God pour out his wrath upon?

Will it be non-believers? No, non-changers. Many were once atheists or agnostics and now confidently call on the Creator.

Perhaps the non-committed? No, again it will be the non-changers. Some who once would not lift a finger for God are now offering their bodies as living sacrifices.

What about the non-friendly? Many have abused relationships in the past but have passed on to a new way of treating people.

Only the non-changer will suffer wrath. The stubborn. The rebellious.

The examples.

"Oh, I've been this way 50 years; I certainly can't change now." Whatever happened to strength and dignity coming with age?

"I have attended this church all my life, and I just couldn't change allegiance now."

Even if your church is wrong?

"I like my philosophy of life. It hasn't hurt me so far."

And where exactly is the word "philosophy" found in the Bible?

Whether you are a teenager or a college student, married or single, retired or on your deathbed, God demands all of us to change. If not, he will call in his wrath.

4) *"The One enthroned in heaven laughs; the Lord scoffs at them. Then he rebukes them in his anger and terrifies them in his wrath"* (Psalm 2:4-5).

It appears there may be a lot of laughing going on up there. Sounds like God might be having a good time.

Here's some good advice. Try to listen carefully for the laughter of heaven because it seems like anger and wrath are usually right behind. Then go make any necessary changes and laugh along.

3) *"The LORD preserves the faithful, but the proud he pays back in full"* (Psalm 31:23).

For all those who refuse to submit to authority, be it spiritual or worldly.

For those who care more for the feelings of an orgasm than the feelings of their partner.

For politicians who take bribes but not phone calls.

For the athlete who makes millions but will not make time to sign autographs.

For the hypocritical church member who shows up on Sunday then slows down his commitment the rest of the week.

More paybacks await these types of people by the impending wrath of God.

2) *"God is a righteous judge, a God who expresses his wrath every day"* (Psalm 7:11).

Some of it you can see, some you cannot. Many rational-

ize away what they *do* see to chance, circumstance or Satan.
But God's wrath is lived out every day. Newspapers report it,
just the wrong headlines.

"Mother Nature Wreaks Havoc on Nation."

Whatever happened to Father God??

1) *"Surely your wrath against men brings you praise, and the
survivors of your wrath are restrained"* (Psalm 76:10).

Thought we might as well end on a good note. Even
God's wrath is designed to get you and me and all other
survivors to change. To be restrained.

To stop getting drunk. Stop cheating. Stop hating. Stop
being immoral. Start loving. Start serving. Start living.

Thank you, God, even for your wrath.

God Is Good

10) *"For the LORD is good and his love endures forever; his
faithfulness continues through all generations"* (Psalm 100:5).

We all search intensely for them. Those faithful someones.
Just one who will keep his word. We pray to find someone
whose vows won't fluctuate like the stock market but instead
remain steady and sturdy through rough and smooth sailing.
When will God not come through? Can you always trust him?

In reality, though, most of us trust just about everything
else. We eat our breakfast cereal and assume no small rocks
are with our Rice Krispies. We pour the milk and trust the
producers have not messed with the cows. We down the medi-
cations confident they are poison-free. But then it happens.

Cars that were not supposed to blow up in an accident,
but did.

Buildings touted as earthquake-safe but were not.

Cyanide-laced aspirin created by monsters and not medicine experts.

I will never forget July 4, 1968. My family and I were
walking to our car following a fireworks display, oblivious to
the upcoming finale only 10 minutes away. To reach our car,

we had to take a footbridge over Lake Sacagawea. The bridge was fairly large and hundreds of us with unswerving trust for its engineers, designers and constructors walked slowly but surely toward its end. But right before I got there, I got the ride of my life. The bridge collapsed, and we all immediately became Humpty Dumpty sympathizers.

I landed on the edge of the water, right next to what must have been a 300-pound, middle-aged woman. (My eyes at the time were as big as they had ever been, so maybe she was 200 pounds. But she was big.) People were tossed into the lake. Moms. Dads. Grandmas. Grandpas. Kids. Babies. Panic was an understatement. Hysteria took over and people were looking to get out to save their lives or get in to save another. Nobody died that night, but there were countless broken bones and many in serious and critical condition.

Since that Independence Day from hell, I have never struggled with bridge trusting. I *have* travelled on the Golden Gate. I have peered over the world's highest suspension bridge in Colorado. I cross bridges daily by foot and by Ford. I honestly cannot remember the last time I prayed that a bridge would last at least until I had safely passed. Why should I? The bridge blunder happened only once.

Why then do we struggle with God-trusting? He has never bottomed out. He has never broken under pressure. Start trusting God again, and get back on your bridge to a happy life.

9) *"Surely God is good to Israel, to those who are pure in heart"* (Psalm 73:1).

We needed that word "surely."

"Are you sure God loves me?"

"Are you sure he is on my side?"

"Are you sure he will help me?"

Do you have a pure heart? Do you desire to do what is right? Are you not living life just for you? If you can answer these questions with a Yes, and repent quickly when temporarily it slips to a No, you simply need to stop doubting and believe.

"Well, maybe God is good to me."
Surely!!
"I think God is good to me."
Surely! Surely! Surely!

8) *"The LORD has made his salvation known and revealed his righteousness to the nations"* (Psalm 98:2).
It has never been like God to keep a secret and never will be.
If something is good, he will let you know how to get it.
If there is forgiveness, he will help you find it.
If there is a heaven, he will honk until you get there.
If there is a playbook, you can get a copy.
And if there is any change, you will be notified.

7) *"For his anger lasts only a moment, but his favor lasts a lifetime"* (Psalm 30:5).
Though absolutely true, many of us would claim the complete opposite. How does *your* heart read it?
"His anger lasts a long time, and I have not felt his favor."
"Oh, about 50-50."
"Maybe around 70-30."
"Somewhere near 90-10."
God shouts "ANGER = 0.001; FAVOR = 99.999."
A few years ago, my wife and I were enjoying a relaxing afternoon, looking for a little time to ourselves after laying our son Bradley, three at the time, down for a nap. A little music, a big fire, a huge plan.
"What is that pounding on the wall?"
"Is Bradley still up?"
We waited and waited some more, but the noise continued. As I climbed the stairs to Bradley's resting place, I knew I was in for a doozy. The smell was obvious. Unfortunately for me, the changer was too. But nothing could prepare me for what I saw upon entering the room. I discovered what I now unaffectionately refer to as modern 'poop' art. My son had done some business in his pants but for some reason had decided to continue dealing. He had taken off his diaper, found a

stick from the closet and was painting on the walls in solid brown.

I was angry. I was very angry. Angry enough so that Bradley knew "poop on a stick" would only occur once. But the anger lasted only a moment. More than to feel my anger, Bradley needed to be taught. He needed to be reinforced that he was loved. He needed to be reminded that Dad would still be Dad. We would still play catch. I would still rent movies for him. My main job now was to spread my favor over this little boy's life.

God cleans up similar messes that we have made with our lives. Is he angered? Yes. For very long? No. Does he instead want to give you his favor? Yes. For how long? Let Psalm 30:5 be your answer to that.

6) *"The heavens declare the glory of God; the skies proclaim the work of his hands. Day after day they pour forth speech; night after night they display knowledge. There is no speech or language where their voice is not heard. Their voice goes out into all the earth, their words to the ends of the world"* (Psalm 19:1-5).

Did you see that? God has been talking to you, and he hasn't missed a day yet!

The skies are not silent. Even the clouds are communicating. Admire them. Discover animals and other objects in their different formations. Ride with them as they float effortlessly across the sky. But most of all, just listen because God is talking. Have you heard the stars shouting at night? Admire them also. Count them if you have the time. Check out all the incredible constellations. Watch them drop, then disappear. You've just heard another powerful message from God. What will you say in return?

What about the rest of creation? It's all there just for you, proclaiming loud and clear that God is good and that he will do anything he can to get our attention, prove to us he's there and then turn us to him.

God speaks to everybody alive on a daily basis. He's the only one capable of talking your ear off and then putting it back on.

5) *"Good and upright is the* LORD; *therefore he instructs sinners in his ways. He guides the humble in what is right and teaches them his way. All the ways of the* LORD *are loving and faithful for those who keep the demands of his covenant"* (Psalm 25:8-10).

The teacher and the tour guide. Able and eager to show off his creation and his truth. A hard-to-find doubleheader. Perhaps God is one of the few tour guides who actually likes his job.

He will gladly explain all about the lion, then warn you about the lion in the devil.

He will introduce you to the sheep and goats, then tell you which one to imitate.

He will analyze the lamb, then teach you the cross.

God wants you to know it all. Hop aboard!

4) *"Taste and see that the* LORD *is good"* (Psalm 34:8).

For years, pumpkin pie for me was "pathetic pie." Oh, I had never tried it. I wouldn't dare. I had seen and smelled the inside of a pumpkin and wanted nothing similar to touch my tongue. But, I had also been taught to be polite and eat what was put before me when dining at others' homes. And I did just that a number of times, eating everything from asparagus to runny scrambled eggs with green peppers, holding my breath and my water glass simultaneously before each daring and disgusting swallow.

One day, the pumpkin pie stared me down. I started my routine, but this time, I felt no pain as I had with most asparagus helpings. Could this be? Could this be good? So I did it. I opened my nostrils, put down my drink and took the Pumpkin Pie Plunge. I ate it normally. Oh, was it good! Proud to say, today, that hands down, pumpkin pie is my #1 choice.

You miss pumpkin pie pleasure, you suffer slightly; you miss God, you suffer eternally. Go ahead. Take a bite. A big one. This verse says you will not be disappointed.

3) *"Yet he was merciful; he forgave their iniquities and did not destroy them. Time after time he restrained his anger and did not stir up his full wrath"* (Psalm 78:38).

How many times for you? I would bet most of us are at least in the thousands. Thank you, God, for not stirring. We would all be cooked.

2) *"How great is your goodness, which you have stored up for those who fear you"* (Psalm 31:19).

How good is God? He's great at it.

How much of that goodness is available to you? Heaven is where the "goods" are stored with reserve deposits so deep we could get supplied minute by minute and millions of blessing buckets would still be available.

1) *"Praise the* LORD, *O my soul; all my inmost being, praise his holy name. Praise the* LORD, *O my soul, and forget not all his benefits—who forgives all your sins and heals all your diseases, who redeems your life from the pit and crowns you with love and compassion, who satisfies your desires with good things so that your youth is renewed like the eagle's. The* LORD *works righteousness and justice for all the oppressed. He made known his ways to Moses, his deeds to the people of Israel: The* LORD *is compassionate and gracious, slow to anger, abounding in love. He will not always accuse, nor will he harbor his anger forever; he does not treat us as our sins deserve or repay us according to our iniquities"* (Psalm 103:1-10).

My favorite Old Testament passage. If the world would only believe its truths.

Have you read this incredible insurance policy lately? Check those benefits once again?

Do you remember where you have come from and what you used to do and be? Check out that complete forgiveness clause.

Remember all the times you got bailed out of invisible jails? Take another close look at the "I can get you out of any pit" package.

Remember when you had no clue and someone dropped huge, heavenly hints? Review that "watched over during wilderness wanderings" addendum to your policy, stop hesitating, and sign on the dotted line.

Hope you enjoyed that long journey through the Bible. 180 verses on God. We have a great God. He will give you the chance to know him, then give you some choices to make.

Chapter Ten

The Chance

"The Lord is not slow in keeping his promise, as some understand slowness. He is patient with you, not wanting anyone to perish, but everyone to come to repentance"

(2 Peter 3:9).

My heart started beating much faster than normal, and it felt as though adrenaline was my middle name. I was so excited, yet also a bit scared, as this was my very first opportunity to set foot inside a state penitentiary, and my first opportunity to present God to an inmate. But not just any inmate. I was there to see Harold Lamont Otey.

Harold (Willie, as he preferred to be called) and his "fight to stay alive" story had become national news material. Nobody had been executed for a crime in more than 30 years in Nebraska, but many believed Willie's death was now imminent.

Willie had been scheduled to die in the electric chair for more than 14 years. He had been convicted of rape and murder in 1977 at the age of 18, but years of point/counterpoint in the Nebraska state and federal courts had brought about numerous stays of execution. Was God waiting for this meeting to take place so he could offer Willie a "last chance" to know him?

I heard about Willie while reading the *Lincoln Journal Star* in 1991. He had just a few days before his "definite"

date with death, so a number of my friends and I began praying for one more delay in hopes that someone could talk
with Willie about God, the Bible and his readiness to meet
his Maker. I desperately desired that "someone" to be me.

We were thrilled upon hearing the good news of another
court-ordered delay. I immediately grabbed my pen and paper and sat down to write a letter of request to Mr. Otey. I
was convinced of God's moving in the situation and told
Willie so, not knowing anything of his belief in a higher power.
I was as honest as I knew how to be and told Willie that he
needed to meet with me to hear information about God that
would change his life, what little he had left of it.

Thrill, part two, came when on a typical mailbox visit, I
noticed a letter from Willie. Surely God was beginning the
unveiling process. Willie (I learned later) received hundreds
of letters each year from death penalty opponents sympathetic with his plight and religious leaders looking for a shot
to "save his soul." He had only responded to a few. Willie,
however, accepted my offer and invited me to come visit.

I went through the typical "get a pass for a prison visit"
ordeal including a scrutinizing background check. But God
was getting in. God was getting involved with Willie Otey.
Now granted, God had always been inside the prison. The
veils are thick there and the demon population dense, so
angels and overtime are necessary. God led me down the
hallways, through numerous checkpoints and finally into the
waiting area.

"Mr. Simmons, you may go in now. Mr. Otey is waiting to
see you."

The time had come. God was about to whisper "I still
love you" in Willie's ear, and I had been selected to make
sure he heard it.

We shook hands and sat down to talk. We were all alone
in a well-lit room sitting across from each other at a table.
And, though I knew guards were within a whisper and sur-
veillance cameras could detect even the slightest of my
twitches, it still came down to me and a man on death row.

My palms were sweaty and my prayers were silent.

"Oh God, more than at any other time, please give me wisdom now."

We began talking, and Willie quickly began sharing his life. He denied the murder, blamed the system and talked of his prison experiences the past 15 years. I doubted his innocence, but knew that, regardless, this man had purchased a veil somewhere in his 32 years, and it needed to be removed before high voltage shocked his body into submission and his soul into account before God.

We became comfortable with each other and laughed together, talked about sports, family and friends, but then spent the last chunk of time looking into the Bible.

Willie believed in a God but was convinced it could not be the God of the Christian persuasion, the God of the Bible. Surely if it was, those "Christians" left in charge of his youth would have been more godly and loving. Surely, his heartfelt, religious experience with Christ during his early teen years would have "stuck" and kept him committed longer than a few months. Surely, his entrance into "Christian" America in the '50s would have introduced him to blacks loving whites, whites loving blacks, equal opportunities and color-blind children.

He missed it. So he missed God. The veil had arrived early, and now Allah was more attractive than God and the Koran more believable than the Bible. I tried with all my heart and with petitional prayers begged God to keep allowing me back into the prison. I was convinced God was not ready to give up.

Willie and I continued to study the Bible. I offered him much of the information you have been reading in this book. I paid Willie a few more visits but, sadly, the veil remained. Though every word and verse we read together was true, Willie's past impression of God had diminished his openness to truth.

I received one final letter from Willie in August 1991. He said he was no longer interested in studying, shed doubt upon my real motives to be his friend and suggested we no longer correspond.

My family and I moved to Cincinnati, Ohio, about two weeks later, but before leaving Lincoln, I would often drive by the prison and pray for Willie. He was still alive, so certainly some hope remained.

Today I read a Chicago newspaper and began to cry. The news from around the nation included a story entitled: "NE-BRASKA EXECUTES FIRST MAN IN 35 YEARS." Harold Lamont Otey was dead. Willie died in the electric chair.

God knew all along of his guilt or innocence in the murder of the Omaha woman in 1977. If guilty, Willie could have been forgiven and joined the likes of David, Moses and Paul—great men over the long haul but weakened for the moment. Or, if innocent, Willie could have been set free. Oh, probably not from prison, but free from the trap of the devil that kept him locked in unbelief of the true God. Free from the disbelief of all the "Christian" hypocrisy he had experienced through the years. And free from the veil he wore to his death.

I know not of God's innermost feelings or thoughts on Willie as he viewed the one he had placed in his mother's womb who was now being placed on an electric chair. But I know that God loved him. And I know that God gave him a great chance to know him.

God gives everybody a chance. Perhaps this book is yours.

Chapter Eleven

The Choice

But if serving the Lord seems undesirable to you, then choose for yourselves this day who you will serve, whether the gods your forefathers served beyond the River, or the gods of the Amorites. But as for me and my household, we will serve the Lord" (Joshua 24:15).

Choices. That describes life. Everything is a choice. Will you get up? When will you get up? Where will you get up? How will you get up?

What's for breakfast? How about eggs? Poached? Scrambled? Over easy, medium or hard-boiled? Maybe cereal? Will it be Wheaties? Cap-n-Crunch? Plain, Peanut Butter or Crunch Berries?

Will you take a shower? For how long? What temperature do you like? What soap do you use? Shampoo?

Will you brush your teeth? Hard or soft bristles? What type of toothpaste? Crest or Colgate? Plain or mint? Will you squeeze from the top or bottom?

What will you wear? Casual, dress or comfortable? What colors? Pants or jeans? Sweater or shirt? Long or short sleeve? Tie or not?

Should you read the paper? Front page? Sports? Local? Funnies? Ads?

Will you go to work? Take a bus? Carpool? Train? Walk? Drive?

Need to get gas? Regular? Unleaded? Supreme? Amoco? Shell? Chevron? Cash? Credit?

Will you take the freeway? Or back way? Will you go fast? Slow? Speed limit?

How hard will you work? Will you smile? Frown? Talk? Will you be silent or sociable? Do you have a "Things to Do" list? What are your priorities? Calls? Letters? Follow-up?

What about lunch? Sack? Go out? Deli? Diner? Burger King? McDonald's? Big Mac? Filet? Fries? Coke? Diet or Regular? For here? To go?

How will you drive home? Same way? Different? Which lane? Which exit? Short way? Fast way?

What's for dinner? Fancy? Simple? Soup? Tomato? Mushroom? Chicken noodle?

Got any after-work plans? How about a date? Work-out? Veg? Sleep?

Will you watch television? What channel? Will it be comedy? Drama? Game? Pro or college?

Should you clean up? Do the dishes? Why not tomorrow?

Go to bed? What time?

Read a book before bed? Mystery? History?

Set alarm for tomorrow? 6:00? 6:15? 6:30?

No wonder we have a hard time finding God. We have so many choices we've learned to choose our own God as well. Yes, prophets have always called the people to make choices about their God. But never about who God was. Only about what they would *do* with the real God.

Joshua said "Do what you want, but I am choosing God."

Elijah refused his audience's wavering and waved the red flag (1 Kings 18:16-21).

Choose.

Jesus preached "You are either for me or against me" (Matthew 12:30).

Choose!

Paul demanded kings and high ranking officials do something with the information they had accumulated over the years about God (Acts 26:24-29).

Choose!

But most of us do not like to choose. Choice means pressure. Commitment. Locked in. Responsibility. We want others to choose for us. What if we make the wrong choice?

But once you have the information, choice is inevitable. By *not* choosing, you choose. By *not* following, you follow something. But you can also choose to not be informed. Ultimately, all the choices we make, we must take responsibility for, and more importantly, we will be held accountable for making.

Some of you have already made the choice. Others still contemplate. For some, what you are about to read will be a review. A reminder. An opportunity to refocus. Recommit. For others, you will learn how your choice to believe in the right God must drastically alter the remaining days of your lives.

Is God holy? Does he pilot the Concorde? Are you just baggage in comparison? Is he above all? Read Chapters Seven, Eight and Nine again if you need to. But choose.

If you decide to say Yes, welcome to a whole new world. No longer can you look down on any type of human being. There is someone above you. No longer will you ignore setting aside time to honor him. No longer will prayer be optional and Bible study basic. You will admire creation and admonish those who do not. You will cringe when you hear his name taken in vain and not in verse. You will respect him for who he is, what he has done and how he has helped you to see both.

Is God all powerful? Can he really do all things? Does he even have limits? Choose. You have seen the facts. Now, you alone are the jury. Choose.

If you decide to say Yes, your world will always keep on changing. No more will you tolerate any self-pity when the wet paper bag has proven to be stronger than your fight. The "I don't think I can change" days are over. The Mom and Dad mold of 18 years no longer will take an equal amount to fix. The little league thinking of life and results will be called up to the major leagues, and you will want your chance to bat. You will expect God to throw you his best, and if you strike out, you will be foaming, chomping and stomping till your next turn around, looking for redemption. You will invite people to church and expect them to come. You will walk with confidence. You will now look for answered prayer like you used to look for another party. You will never expect second best but expect the best in a second. Boldness will be an expectation, not a goal. You will look to God, wait for God, run with God, work with God and succeed with God.

Is God good? Or is he just a pretty decent deity? Is everything he does done with our best interest in mind? You have already read. Now you choose. Here we go again.

If you said Yes, your gratitude list will grow with each passing day, and you will look for the light at the end of the tunnel to free you and not for the bats to fear. You will shout "Whoa!" to the "Woe is me"s. You will stop complaining at work, at home, on the road and in the church. You will be the unofficial, unauthorized, unelected but totally qualified chair of the positive-thinking committee in your community, work place, neighborhood and family. You will call out the spiritual cops when you cop an attitude and surrender without resistance. You will work to solve problems and not to analyze them. You will thank God, trust God, and team with God to stamp out negativity, whining and complaining.

Is God caring? Will he take time for you and me? Is he distant or at hand? Is he harsh or sensitive? Is he willing to understand or uncaring? Are we an unwelcomed guest? What do you think? Choose.

If you say Yes, you're in luck. You get to start caring for others and find the real meaning of life and, in the meantime, give the world the real meaning of God. You will look to convince the skeptics. You will touch a leper. You will tell your parents you love them regularly. You will cry. You will want to attend funerals and weddings and weep with those who weep and rejoice with those who rejoice. You will stop and thank God for his care signs and sign up to care for others. You will hurt for your boss's dilemmas. You will hurt when told No to a church invitation. You will search for a lost sheep and provide extra food for those you leave behind. You will pray to see a world full of Christians and have a suitcase in hand in case you are called to go anywhere.

Is God hard-line? Is there a bottom line? Are there lines man cannot cross? Chosen yet? Getting a little tougher now but still well worth it. Choose!

If Yes, welcome to the world of a true Father. "How far can I get" will turn into "How far can I go to prove my purity?" You will be more careful and less carefree. You will develop a "play it safe" mentality and call others to do the same. Tax forms will be correct. Laws will be honored. Government officials will be supplicated for, not slandered. You will challenge someone's claims to salvation while not judging them, never assuming it to be true. You will prove by Bible and not by background. You will read more Bible and less commentary. You will change churches, change tradition, and change your mind if that's what it takes to match it with the Bible. Wedding gowns will be white and really mean something. You will discipline your kids, train your kids, and lead your kids. You will seek help, get help, and get back on track. You will confess your sin, and work to eliminate all possible temptations. You will even give up your life if it means living forever.

Is God a just God? Will he punish? Is there a hell? Does God get angry? How often? Or is God passive, flexible and compromising? Is hell merely a scare tactic? Choose!

If you say Yes, welcome to a world of fear. Oh, not all those things you have feared up until now, just the one thing you have not: God. You will fear. You will seek to persuade the stubborn. You will call back a third time to see if your neighbor wants to study the Bible. A fourth time. Fifth. You will not run from a rebuke or analyze it, but heed it. You will think about hell more often than before and never dream someone into heaven who is headed for hell. Not Mom, Dad, Grandma, Grandpa, neither the dead nor the living.

I met Vince Hawkins in January 1991. Vince was an impressive young man, 6 feet 1 inch, 210 pounds, slender but strong. Vince was one of the starting wingbacks for the perennial national football powerhouse, the Nebraska Cornhuskers. He grew up in the projects of New Orleans with a religious family, excelled in high school athletics and then started as a tailback for two years at a Community College in Spokane, Washington, before coming to Nebraska with a full-ride athletic scholarship. I liked Vince from the outset, but I had a job to do. God had called me to help change this man's life. To do that, though, I knew I must change this young man's god. He was blind. He had on a thick veil.

Vince had come to Nebraska as a god of sorts. Many Nebraska coeds live for the day they can date or do favors for a Nebraska star athlete. Vince was not one to disappoint them. Vince was cocky, cool and confident, and he knew it. What he did not know was that he was confused as well. He had purchased a new Bible only one month earlier in Florida during a Citrus Bowl trip but had read very little since that time. This was not surprising at all, especially due to the fact it was a King James Bible (hardeth to understandeth version). Nothing personal, but Vince at the time would barely read a 20th-century Living Bible, let alone a 16th-century relic. But at least he had one.

When we planted the church in Lincoln, my dream had been to quickly convert a Cornhusker player. I had other goals, of course, but loving college football like I did, and seeing a player become a disciple, well, little would have been better. I wanted Vince to make it. But I wanted more for him to know God. Then he would have a fighting chance.

I knew Vince was extremely immoral (I guessed, but it was not a very risky guess), so our very first time together we talked about the birds and the bees—that his way of living was for the birds, and if he did not change, God would sting him. I laid it out as best I could. He did not like it at all. Nobody does. We studied for about two hours that day, and after he left, I was shaking. (That happens to me whenever I find myself in an intense spiritual battle). Would he come back? Would he still study? Yes.

Yes. But there was much more to study.

Vince would have to choose a holy God. He no longer could be a "big man on campus." Instead of seeking his *own* honor, he must seek to honor God.

Vince had to choose a powerful God. He had to believe that though he had never been pure since he could remember, God could change him radically, and purity would become his strength.

He also had to choose a good God. Why the projects? Why the troubles? Why the five-year-old son he loved but could rarely see? Why the prejudice? Why the stares on the streets of Lincoln? Why didn't he know his real dad? Was God really good like the Bible said?

Vince had to choose a caring God. He would have to start hoping the best for his teammates, even those vying for his position. No more trash-talking would be allowed with the opponents. No more selective association with the campus elite. Would Vince now love and serve even the unathletic nerd?

Now the toughest test. Accepting a hard line God. His previous religion was not founded in Scripture. Would he see it? He was to be at church Sunday mornings and whenever else the body met together. Would he be there? Sunday during the season is the college football player's Sabbath day— the time to sleep in and sleep off the game the day before and the girls the night before. Some of his coaches had concerns about what they considered "over involvement" in the church and made bold attempts to keep him from studying with us. He continued.

Vince had to choose a God of justice and wrath. He had to accept that there was a hell, and he was heading there. He needed to take that last leap of faith. He knew that if he did, it then would become his task to testify to others on the team. The choice was tough. He knew what was right. He knew who God was. Now he had to choose. Day after day, Aaron (who lived three doors down from Vince in the dorms) and I continued to urge Vince to choose. He did not. The battle was heavy. Even the angels had on helmets.

It was February 12, 12:30 a.m. and about 10 degrees wind-chill and had been that way for days. Vince and Aaron and I were wrapping up our Bible study, and, frankly, I had re-signed myself to preparing for the next day's battle.

"Let's do it," Vince said. "I'm ready to be baptized."

I think I said "Are you sure?" about 12 times, one time each for every day Vince had said No prior to that. But I knew he was ready. He had learned. He had labored. Now he was choosing.

We had a horse trough in our basement, so I assumed Vince would opt for the safe, warmer waters of salvation.

"Let's go to Holmes Lake," he said.

I always ask someone where they want to be baptized in case they have a special place in mind. I figured it was a done deal. It was. But it was Vince's done deal. Aaron and I went down to the half frozen lake, found some deep enough water, ran out with Vince and both of us buried him and raised him up to a new life (Romans 6:1-6).

It was on our way to the baptism that Vince uttered a statement that reconvinced me he was ready. That he under-stood. That only God mattered. That the veil was gone.

"Now isn't this amazing?" he said. "Here it is 2:00 a.m. in Lincoln, Nebraska. I'm getting baptized in a frozen lake, and I'm doing it all with two white guys."

Way to go Vince. You chose wisely. By the way, Vince is doing great. He is married now to a beautiful disciple hav-ing kept a pure relationship intact with her for more than two years. He has helped two other UNL football players and other Nebraska athletes to know God and now leads one of the campus ministries in the church in Denver.

He chose! So can you. You can choose the horse trough over the lake. You can choose a jacuzzi for all that matters. But there is still only *one* God to choose.

Chapter Twelve

The Battle

Be self-controlled and alert. Your enemy the devil
prowls around like a roaring lion looking for someone to
devour. Resist him, standing firm in the faith, because
you know that your brothers throughout the world are
undergoing the same kind of suffering"

(1 Peter 5:8-9).

There goes that devil again. So, you choose, you make great decisions, you change your life and he *still* wants to know if you would like a veil. Five days, five years or five decades later, the offer will always remain. That is how he devours. He figures that if he did it once, chances are good he may be able to do it again. *Do not let him!* Stay in the battle!

The parable of the sower talks about veils. (Read Mark 4:1-20.) One man kept his original. Two got rid of theirs, then bought them back. Only one got rid of his permanently. The good news is, he helped many others to burn theirs, as well. But all were a part of the battle.

The battle comes from the pressures of life. The testing that God promised would come. (See Deuteronomy 8:1-5.) The worries, cares, desires and demons who flaunt themselves, flirt, then fasten themselves to your spiritual eyes. Oh no, you're blind again! You forgot to resist!

It will take resistance. Saying No to a car salesman is often a challenge. Expert veil salesmen are much more slippery and convincing. Resistance will take effort. Time. Patience. And most importantly, power. *A greater power,* because demons will be pushing you back to your old way of thinking and, consequently, if you're not careful, your old way of life, your old veil.

Where will the battles be won and lost? Largely with your schedule. Making absolutely sure you make absolutes about time spent with God. The word is meant to be read daily. How many times do you hear a great message and one day later forget 98% of the content? You remembered the punchline (because it was so bad) but can't remember the points. So many distractions. So many demons of bad memory. So many enemies eager to erase truths. You must reserve time to read and make that time as sacred as the Bible itself. Read some more. Read the verses over and over again. Memorize. Meditate. Make it happen.

You also must reserve time to pray. Take plenty of time to get away and tell God how the veil might be coming back and how you need strength to say No to the next offer and how you desperately want to help others get rid of theirs.

Get fellowship. Don't just *attend* church; go there with a plan to encourage. Take notes during the sermons. Check the source by checking your Source. Talk truth with other veil-haters. Look for any signs of invisible veils on them, and ask them to look you over as well.

Get busy. The more spare time you have, the more opportunity Satan has to sucker you into a sale.

Get involved. Reach out. Help the homeless. Visit the sick. Find out what needs to be done in the church and go do it.

Grow. Don't be content with where you are, but look ahead to where you will be. And when you get there, look ahead some more. Before you know it, you'll be in heaven. But remember: *If you do not grow, you die.* It is a simple, universal truth that few want to apply to the spiritual world. Peter describes those who do not grow as being nearsighted and blind (2 Peter 1:3-9). Sounds like a veil might be the problem. Are you closer to God than you were last year? Are you stronger? Are you happier? Are you bolder? Are you more confident? Are you more like Jesus? Examine yourself regularly, get to some good spiritual doctors, get some X-rays and get the help you need.

Get ready for the tests. They're inevitable. They're godly. Tests are the best way for God (and us!) to discover our heart's true condition. Study for the tests. Practice. Have people quiz you. Talk about how you will do. Make vows on what you will do.

Maybe the test will be a sickness and joy level will determine your score.

Maybe the test will be the death of a loved one and your conviction on their eternal condition will mean pass or fail.

Or maybe it will be an old girlfriend who wanders back into the picture looking to frame you. Will you get other women involved to study with her? Will you refuse that dinner at her place, alone and risky? Your decisions will determine your grade.

Maybe your child will leave God and you will be tempted to leave room for bitterness and "I can't believe you're doing this to me"s.

It may be a financial issue. It may be unanswered prayer.

Whatever "it" is, if you are not prepared, "it" will eat you alive. Devour you.

You must persevere through persecution. You will get some (2 Timothy 3:12). Some will turn into a lot. It is predicted and promised and can, in an unbelievably effective way, pick out the real God-lovers. I have seen too many leave when the heat was on, to take the heat off on this point. Others, however, survive, grow and flourish.

I take my hat off to all the college students who chose to forego a four-year parental tuition waiver rather than forsake their God. Mom and Dad said to stop going to *that* church, and you refused. You love Mom and Dad, but you now work two jobs, take fewer credits and will take an extra year to graduate. Take a bow. God is applauding.

To all the high school students who are the only, or one of a mere few committed Christians on their entire campus. You try to fit in, but it is real hard. You are cool, but you love Christ, and you are not looking for the perfect one to "do it with" that first time. You have decided to wait until you are married. You don't date anybody on campus. You decided to date God-lovers only. You have chosen to fish in one pond, while others catch regularly in bountiful waters nearby. You stuff a Bible in your crowded locker. Others bring pornography. You *read* yours. They just look. High school heroes receiving heaven's highest praise.

To the single mom refusing to be known as a victim. She is Mom *and* Dad for now. She is "looking" but not compromising. She gives consistently and complains inconsistently. She is at all the church services, all the Bible studies and looking for more. Her critics says she uses the church as a crutch and a baby-sitter. She merely admits she is weak without God and loves for her kids to learn about him. Her parents may not understand; her kids may not understand. But she understands, and that will have to do for now.

The wives married to the non-believers. Some spouses come to church, but only occasionally. Some never come. Some make their wives' lives difficult for coming. Some of the wives get treated right. Some get ignored as a payback. Some get slapped. Some get sworn at. Some come to church crying, but they still come. Then they bite their lip hard and go home with a vow to memorize, then live by 1 Peter 3:1-6. Then they fix dinner, clean the house, and meet all the family's needs. They receive no cards in return. No flowers. No thanks. But vows were spoken and will never be broken. They pray boldly and daily for their husbands to be saved. They would exchange it for anything. They sit through sermons pointing to great marriages and only wonder. They watch husband and wife hold hands at church as they pray and take communion together. They fold theirs. They wonder if their children will want to follow Mom or Dad. Private pain. Private persecution. Perseverance will be rewarded.

Hats off to Tyrone Byrd, as well. I met Tyrone in April 1991 in the Nebraska football locker room following the annual spring game. Vince Hawkins (Chapter Ten) had been reaching out to Tyrone trying to set up a Bible study, and he agreed to get with me. I figured it would be Vince Part 2. I was close. Tyrone had a little more understanding and conviction, but was lost nonetheless.

During our third time together I told Tyrone bluntly what his eternal destiny was according to the Bible. Tyrone was not happy with me or what I had just told him. Would he repent or run me over? Would he take it like a man or tackle me like a dummy? Would he remember this was a Bible study and not a Bowl game? I needed Tyrone to remain calm.

His freshman year he was named Big 8 Newcomer of the Year, and then added an outstanding sophomore year to his credentials. He was a Big 8'er. I was a big eater. Tyrone had been tested at 4% body fat. I had never been tested before then, but undoubtedly would have had a little more pinched than that. Now granted, I did outweigh him by 10 pounds, but that would have been my only advantage. He was a solid 185 pounds, a starting free safety, and I was a soft, 195-pounder who regularly looked for safety.

Tyrone now shares of how unbelievably close he came to laying me out physically after I laid him out spiritually. Hopefully Vince, who was also involved in the study, would have intervened and saved me from future blows, but certainly one would have squarely landed. I thank God the angels landed first.

Well, we worked through that bump, and about a week later Tyrone was baptized in our basement horse trough. By that time I was open to Holmes Lake (because it was the middle of May and a nice 80-degree day in Lincoln! Funny how the Lord works!).

After a decent junior year, Tyrone received First Team All-Big 8 honors his senior year in 1992, while helping his team earn another Orange Bowl berth. He set the all-time record for tackles at his position and had 11 career interceptions as a Husker. One of those interceptions came on national television in November of 1992 against Kansas which he brought back for a touchdown. Another came against 1993 Heisman Award Winner, Charlie Ward, in the 1993 Orange Bowl.

Tyrone was a very talented athlete and had huge aspirations for playing professional football. Most of those "in the know" thought he could make it. Most importantly, he did too. He was touted to be a middle-round draft choice; some believed he might go higher, others a bit lower. But that would mean money. Fame. Opportunity. He could fulfill a life-long dream, help his family, and perhaps help other professional football players to throw off their veils.

But one March evening during spring break, Tyrone was headed for the fight of his life. You may remember the night. ESPN called it the "Night of Tragedy." That same night, Steve Olin and Tim Crews, Cleveland Indians pitchers, were killed in a boating accident in Florida and Bob Ojeda, also of the Indians, was critically injured. Only hours later, Tyrone was in central New Mexico, a few hours from his family and a spring break visit. The draft would be next month, so excitement was in the air for the Byrd family. While asleep in the passenger seat, his best friend, Alston, fell asleep at the wheel temporarily and overcompensated when he awoke. Consequently, the car left the ground, then landed and rolled numerous times before coming to rest.

Life Flight helicopters came to the accident scene and took Tyrone and Alston to an Albuquerque hospital. Alston was pronounced dead on arrival from massive head injuries. Tyrone was still alive. And alert. According to him, he wasn't hurt that bad, but X-rays showed a broken neck and shattered bones underneath his right eye. He would live, but dreams of pro football would die.

I got a call about 11:00 a.m. that next morning telling me that Alston was dead, and Tyrone was in critical condition. I had just gotten home from an untimely and unjoyful visit to my dentist who had removed my four wisdom teeth and extracted another tooth. Though groggy from all the medication, I knew I had to go. I hopped on the next available flight and arrived in Albuquerque.

Tyrone looked better than I thought he would. He was scheduled for surgery on his eye that night, but nothing major. Or, so we thought. During surgery, Tyrone developed an allergic reaction to the anesthesia and stopped breathing. Doctors tried reviving him and subsequently one of his lungs was punctured. Fluid spilled in and death was knocking at his door. About 3:00 a.m. that morning we got a call at the hotel to pray for Tyrone as things looked bleak. Vince and I got on our knees, along with Jay Kelly, the leader of the Lincoln Christian Church at the time. We begged God, and we believe he answered ours and others' prayers as Tyrone healed.

In the midst of his recovery, confusion reigned. Tyrone's family had not been too positive about his commitment to the church and, through circumstances to this day I'm still confused about, many of us were not allowed to see him, nor were the many letters sent to him from across the country being delivered. He wondered where we were. Why were we gone? Where was his girlfriend, Kelly? Satan was flaunting the veil even in the critical care unit. What a plan. It was the only place he figured he might be able to get this young, talented, but faithful man of God.

I had one last opportunity to see Tyrone. It was to inform him that Alston had died. He began to sob and his breathing and condition worsened. Doctors had OK'd me telling him, but you can imagine the guilt and worry I felt.

More confusion and religious disagreement with family and friends ensued until Tyrone was able to talk to a disciple from Lincoln on the telephone and straighten out most of the mess. In the next few months, though, insurance problems, bankruptcy due to unpayable medical costs, having to drop out of spring semester at UNL, and further family conflicts proved Satan was still hanging on. But so was Tyrone. He had overcome. He grew. He got stronger. He healed.

He is back. He has graduated, and he now lives in Los Angeles. No, he is not playing for the Raiders or the Rams, but pursuing a greater dream—to work in the full-time ministry.

A best friend died. A promising professional football career aborted. Family conflicts. Physical pain. Financial insecurities. Friends apparently abandoning him when he needed them most. The battle was hard and long.

There will be more. But for now, Tyrone is fine. He's a victor. A success story. Because of his spirit, his drive and his determination, certainly Tyrone would have excelled on the field. For now, his battles will be elsewhere.

Thanks for the inspiration, Tyrone. You made God proud. You refused the veil.

Chapter Thirteen

The End

"*Therefore, my dear brothers, stand firm. Let nothing move you. Always give yourselves fully to the work of the Lord, because you know that your labor in the Lord is not in vain*"

(1 Corinthians 15:58).

Our last breath. We'll all take it. Death has reigned since Adam and rains on life's parades daily. It is no respecter of persons.

A 25-year-old NBA superstar. A homeless alcoholic. A Hollywood legend. A mill worker.

Young. Old. Middle-aged.

The reasons are numerous. Accidents. Disease. Wars. Murders. Heart attacks. Aneurysms.

Though taxes may come and go, death is here to stay.

In 1981, I was doing an internship for a local newspaper to complete my journalism degree requirements and was given as one of my many tasks the responsibility of writing the obituaries. The column appeared in every paper. Death was everywhere, even in a small Washington community of 20,000 residents. My job was to report the facts. The funeral homes supplied the information, and I was to contact them regularly for updates.

I remember visualizing that my name would one day appear in the obituary column. A young reporter would call the funeral home where my body was and secure accurate information about my life, my achievements, my relatives and my final resting place.

Your name will appear as well. You and I will have a funeral. People will come. People will cry. Someone will probably say something nice about you. People will mourn for you. They will file one by one past your casket to view your lifeless body. They will remember you. They will tell stories of what it used to be like when you were around. But none of it will matter. Only God's analysis of you and your life will matter. And your analysis of God before your death will make all the difference.

Die without a veil. Please.

I wish you could have met Chip Stone. Chip was a high school All-American swimmer from Texarkana, Texas, and received a scholarship to the University of Nebraska. A shoulder injury and ensuing surgery ended that short-lived career, but Chip came to Nebraska to go under the water, not race across it. He was baptized into Christ in January of 1991, only four days after beginning to study the Bible. Chip always wanted to be his best for God and at times even needed to be told that God had more grace than he was giving him credit for. But what a heart! In a world where people look to get away with the maximum, Chip was a pleasure to lead.

I left Lincoln in August 1991 for Cincinnati but have so many fond and funny memories of my time with Chip. Chip had little or no manual dexterity and his lack of coordination was humorous to observe. He knew it and laughed along. If you were down and wanted a good laugh, all you had to do was take Chip to the bowling alley. A left-hander, he would walk down the approach (about as crooked as a drunk on a white line for a police officer), raise his left elbow, what seemed like two feet above his head, and heave a 16-pound UFO halfway down the lane. (I believe 46 was his top score while I was there.) I doubt the following years brought much improvement. He would have the whole bowling alley watching. I think the owners pondered hiring him for family entertainment.

One time on a trip to Texas to visit family, Chip was pulled over by a police officer under the suspicion of drunk driving. He failed every test without a drop of alcohol in his system. Saying the alphabet backwards was not his forte. The "fast as you can finger to the nose" test held out no hope for Chip to pass. Nevertheless, he was able to convince the officer of his sobriety. No doubt angels nearby were cutting up, and perhaps even God from a distance was laughing.

Chip grew quickly and was very effective in helping others become Christians. He had helped convert some people in his dorm and a former swimming teammate and longed to share his love for God with his family, whom he loved and respected greatly.

Chip's real name was Alston. He took his last breath on that New Mexico highway while taking Tyrone to see his family. The lost world had lost one of its brightest hopes.

Chip's funeral came much earlier than everybody expected and sooner than everybody wanted. But the good news is, he died veilless.

Zack Hill was another gem. A convert to Christianity in the early '80s, he had remained faithful to God through many ups and downs. Zack married in 1990, and he and his wife, Elaine, were two of the 25 who moved with us to Lincoln in 1991. Zack was one of those guys who nobody knew was doing much except those he was doing it for. A secret servant. A thin man with thick skin. A slight man with a huge heart. Zack had always dreamed of the day his brother or any family member would become Christians. He often said it may take something drastic to get their attention. That something was cancer of the liver. Zack's liver.

I saw Zack about a week before he died. You could see and feel almost every bone in his body, and his hair was gray and thinning. He looked so much older than I had remembered but still very much in love with God and void of a veil. Just a few weeks before he died, Zack got to see his brother become a disciple. God showed him his dream then showed him the way home.

And Chip is home, too. He must have quite the mansion. Undoubtedly, a bowling alley is in his basement. Maybe he's scored more than 100 by now. (That would be heaven for Chip.) Surely there's a pool nearby where Chip swims with a perfect shoulder in championship form. And on the entrance to his already completed mansion, a solid-gold plaque reading as follows:

"Well done good and faithful servant. Enter the joy of your master."

Well done, Chip. Well done.

I guess fairy tales can come true. But all fairy tale participants have one thing in common. No veils. Make today your "once upon a time" beginning. Welcome to happily ever after.

The End

Epilogue

oday's newspaper will make its best attempt to discourage you.

Wars abroad will be brought into your front room. More reports of famine will be broadcast.

Politicians and their reputations will be left in question.

Religious leaders will have been involved in acts even the unreligious would disdain.

The police blotter will appear, as well as the county courthouse reports. More reports of drunk driving and unfulfilled marriage vows.

Buy the paper if you want, but don't buy into the lie you'll be tempted to believe—"The world is a mess, and there is absolutely nothing you can do about it."

Keep reading. Keep growing. Keep changing. Keep believing. Keep the devil at a distance. Our world is too important to just watch disintegrate. Five billion plus people will someday stand before God and give an account.

So put your newspaper down, get your Bible out, learn about God, and learn from God what you can do to make a difference.

Just in case the veil is still nearby and you've somehow erased the "true God" tapes, join me for a quick review.

Intelligent. Architect. Founder. Maker. Originator. Knowledgeable. Capable. Honorable. Dependable. Reliable. Impeccable. Indisputable. Invincible. Complete. Wholehearted. Aware. Thoughtful. Kind. Considerate. True. Real. Trustworthy. Patient. Humble. Honest. Forgiving. Loving. Perfect. Wise. Powerful. Poised. Good. Helpful. Holy. Delightful. Strong. Caring. Compassionate. Responsive. Sympathetic. Tender. Warm. Forbearing. Merciful. Gracious. Attentive. Generous. Genuine. Sincere. Upright. Long-suffering. Composed. Just. Right.

Devoted. Loyal. Affectionate. Faithful. Flawless. Excellent. Absolute. Mighty. Competent. Dynamic. Great. Support- ive. Steady. Collected. Useful. Unblemished. Hallowed. Divine. Supreme.

And most of all, AVAILABLE!

Though you will never comprehend his greatness, know- ing him will make for a great life. Though you will never understand his entire wisdom, wisdom says, "Go after what you can," and start filling up a typically empty life. Though you never understand exactly how much God loves you, you will love what you can conclude. Though you can never as- certain all the power he possesses, there is great power in relying on the one with all the muscle and might.

God is amazing. He loves you and looks to lead you to victory in this life and a victory celebration in heaven. Be- fore we finish, however, God asks you to look in the mirror one last time. Do you see a veil? Is it still there? Are there any threads remaining? Or, are you beginning to believe again? Do you believe perhaps for the first time? Do the phrases "following God" and "exciting life" seem compat- ible once again? Now go make up for lost time and start living and looking forward to an eternity with our great God.

Discipleship Publications International invites you
to share with us your response to this book.
We want to know what is most helpful to you and
what other materials you would find useful.
Write to:

Discipleship Publications International
Attn: Managing Editor
One Merrill Street
Woburn, MA 01801